A Bedtime Poem
For Every Day Of The Year

First published in Great Britain in 2006 by:
Anchor Books
Remus House
Coltsfoot Drive
Peterborough
PE2 9JX
Telephone: 01733 898102
Website: www.forwardpress.co.uk
All Rights Reserved
© Copyright Contributors 2006
SB ISBN 1-84418-426-9

Disclaimer
Anchor Books has maintained every effort
to publish poems that will not cause offence.
Any stories, events or activities relating to individuals
should be read as fictional pieces and not construed
as real-life character portrayal.

Foreword

Anchor Books warmly invites you to this showcase of a unique compilation of classic and modern verse for children. Since establishing in 1992 we have been proud to be able to produce quality anthologies sharing these talented works for everyone to enjoy. Anchor Books prides itself on printing poets from all backgrounds of life with stories and anecdotes and general views on life from a wide age range. Poems published featue classic and traditional mostly rhyming verses, as they are family orientated.

This book features fantastically creative and beautiful verse by poets where each poem has been allotted to a day of the year. We were enchanted by the thousands of entries our contributors had kindly submitted for this special book. Our selection procedure was a lengthy process with poems that were amusing and charming.

The poems in this book are enchanting tales featuring fairies and monsters and childlike dreams which will be a pleasure for elders to read to children or for the children themselves to read and delight in at bedtime.

Contents

Abigail Cowley 199	Avril Jessey 245
A Blakemore 363	Barbara Hampson 233
Aderemi Adegbite 201	Barbara Lucy Hosken 208
Alan C Brown 130	Barrie Singleton 246
Alan Glendinning 129	Belinda Abraham 343
Alan Hawthorn 388	Bernard Brady 353
Alan Millard 357	Bernard Fyles 289
Albert Russo 84	Bill Eden 247
Alex Brown (aged 8) & Mummy	Bob Fiddaman 390
aged a lot more) 151	Brenda Maple 330
Alison Pickard 173	Brian Frost 66
Allen Beil 240	Brian McInally 194
Allison Bell 125	Camille Metcalfe 118
Alvin Creighton 214	Carly Dugmore 64
Amy Clayton 86	Carmen Emmanuelle 112
Andrew J Ball 285	Carol Don Ercolano 340
Andy Pitcher 379	Carrie-Anne Fry 325
Andy Wheeler 218	Catherine Bradbury 320
Angela Bullock 315	Charlotte McMullen 179
Angela Dolphin 83	Cheryl Gordon 298
Anna Bayless 265	Chris Gutteridge 117
Anna Green 362	Christine Renee Parker 360
Anne Elibol 263	Christopher Higgins 321
Anne Mitchell 341	Claire Louise Stendall 292
Anne Rolfe-Brooker 72	Claire Tupholme 365
Annette Griffiths 76	Clement Clarke Moore 394
Annie McKimmie 75	Colin Wallace 351
Anthony Hayward 143	Connie Anderson 296
Ashleigh Rice (13) 338	Connie Moseley 345
Ashley O'Keefe 387	Cora Barras 260
Atiyah Wazir 352	Courtney Marshall 168

Name	Page
Craig Shuttleworth	124
C R Slater	326
Crystal Waters	169
C Thornton	282
Daniela Schwarz	209
Danielle Eyres	310
Dan McPheat	368
Daphne Cornell	34
Daphne Fryer	142
Darryl Benson	238
Dave Palmer	306
David Anderson	349
David Brown	19
David Chapman	210
David Charles	228
David Maidment	36
David Whitney	144
Dawna Mechelle	402
Debbie Storey	153
Deborah Hall	227
D E Cornell	43
Deirdre Lubbe	17
Denise Pettitt	182
Denis Martindale	250
D G W Garde	324
Diana Daley	249
Diane Bowen	21
Di Bagshawe	156
Dickon Springate	248
Di Mundell	71
D M Brighton	356
D M Neu	197
Donald John Tye	212
Don Goodwin	145
Donna Salisbury	332
Don Woods	318
Edward S Wall	348
Eileen Bailey	23
Eileen Barlow	290
Eileen Kyriacou	121
Eileen McTeir	16
Eileen O'Brien	230
Eileen Peggs	163
Eileen W O'Brien	287
Elizabeth Love	33
Elizabeth Morton	69
Ella Wright	93
E Marjorie Bright	216
E M Caiger Gray	22
Emelie Buckner	136
Emma Lockyer	154
E Wogden	106
Fiona Spotswood	132
F K McGarry	354
Fleur Pyves	255
Frances Gibson	371
Freda Clayton	100
Gary Bills	364
George Coombs	244
Georgina A Lord	231
Georgina Paraskeva	148
Gerald S Bell	358
Gerard Melia	200
Gillian Hesketh	192
Gillian Mullett	128
Glenda Doller	277
Glenda Evison	20
Glenwyn Peter Evans	305
Glenys Chapman	203
Gordon Andrews	147
Graeme Illingworth	347
Harry Lyons	50
Hayley Hopkins	68
Hazel Calpee	221
Hazel Davies	115
Hazell Dennison	14

Name	Page
Hazell Dennison	104
Heather Killingray	170
Helen McKinlay	297
Helen Moll	393
Helen Scott	232
Helen Smith	47
Irene Pickering	378
Jackie Davies	288
Jackie Williams	383
Jacqueline Ibbitson	236
James Kitchener	111
James S Cameron	224
Jane Bower	126
Janet Fludder	302
Janet Greenwood	384
Janet M Pinto	331
Jan Harris	114
Janice Mitchell	161
Jan Janik	189
Jan Oskar Hansen	127
Jay Berkowitz	77
Jean McGovern	317
Jean Selmes	323
Jeff Northeast	294
Jennifer Densham	268
Jennifer H Fox	322
Jessica Bartlett	135
Jessica Shakespeare	374
Jessie Bruce	267
J H Jenkins	327
Jim Gordon	375
Jim Staton	370
J M Gallen	63
Joan May Wills	382
Joanne Hale	400
John Clarke	108
John Coombes	329
John Henry Foley	304
John Owen Freeth	392
John Thompson	397
Jolanta Gradowicz	272
Josephine Reading	187
Joyce Gale	314
Joyce Graham	220
Joyce Newton	39
Joyce Warden	399
Joy Green	190
Joy Saunders	309
Joy Weare	258
J P Henderson-Long	196
Judith Watts	102
Julia Gallego	284
Julie Channer	377
Julie L Preston	350
Julie Trainor	178
J Windle	152
Karen Beedon	25
Karen Cormick	41
Karl Jakobsen	166
Karl Mcroor	30
Katherine Gallagher	183
Kathleen Potter	175
Kathryn Cook	366
Kay Jones	335
Ken Lou	269
Kerrie Wood	184
Kerri Fordham	312
Kevin Baskin	259
Kevin McSkelly	376
Kim Taylor	31
Kirsty Louise Phillips	344
L A G Butler	140
Laura Clarke	35
Laura Föst	293
Lee Allen	15
Lee A Marsh	177

Leo Cappel	222
Leon Adjarkoh (10)	98
Leon Rafnson	372
Lesley Elaine Greenwood	276
Leslie de la Haye	229
Leslie Rocker	65
Liane Bell	32
Linda Howitt	55
Linda Knight	29
Lisa Oldham	207
Lisa Shambrook	80
Liz Cozens	27
Lorelei Long	359
Louise Foster	234
Louise Hercules	141
Louise Smith	280
Lyndsay Lynch	262
Lynne Walden	172
Lynsey Hawkins	334
Magdalene Chadwick	311
Malcolm Wilson Bucknall	237
Marc E Wright	122
Margaret B Baguley	256
Margaret Carl Hibbs	367
Marjorie Busby	264
Mark Guy	131
Mark Paddington	162
Marlene Parmenter	101
Martina Radford	52
Martin James Banasko	308
Mary Buckley-Clarke	300
Mary Frances Mooney	281
Mary Younger	171
Megan Wileman (12)	205
Michael Campbell	56
Michele Howe	59
Michelle Borrett	386
Mike Tracey	266
M Rae	160
M Wilcox	211
Naomi Thorne	94
Nava Semel	60
N D Wood	333
Nick Kitching	97
Nicola Hopkins	191
Nik Perring	242
Norman Bissett	90
O Monica Fisher	253
Owen Robert Cullimore	380
Pamela Evans	275
Pamela Gormley	46
Paola Borella	202
Patricia Carter	146
Patricia Johnson	37
Patsy Goodsir	226
Pat Watson	137
Paula Slack	54
Paul Green	58
Pauline Andrews	303
Pauline Boncey	157
Pauline Giffen	336
Paul O'Boyle	107
Paul Spender	158
Peggy Briston	176
Peggy Netcott	301
Penny Smith	13
Pete Hazell	279
Peter Davies	78
Pete Williams	99
Philip Anthony McDonnell	252
Philip Sanders	319
P Hoddinott	96
Pip Hill	73
P M Stone	57
Polly Cordell	28
Rachel Gowdy	123

Rachel Hobson	307	S J Davidson	110
Raghda Al-Jassar	88	S Mullinger	138
Rebecca Guest	49	S Mullinger	239
Rex Andrews	391	Sparkle Andrews	204
Richard J Bradshaw	105	Stephanie Teasdale	273
Richard Mills	342	Stephen Page	278
Richard Stead	18	Steve Kettlewell	74
Rich Roach	206	Steve Prout	339
Rick Matiowski	398	Stevie Gregg (8)	286
R M Hughes	385	Sue Hansard	42
Robert Carson	139	Sue Smith	316
Robert H Quin	89	Susan Carter	85
Roger N Taber	164	Susan Gordon	103
Roma Davies	79	Tanzia Haq	251
Ronald Moore	291	T D Green	188
Rosemary Davies	91	Terry Daley	133
Rosemary Keith	257	Tholana Ashok Chakravarthy	213
Roy Tuvey	155	Thomas Dickinson	82
Russell Harvey Mortimer	328	Thomas Ian Graham	120
Ruth Clark	217	T J Shaw	174
Ryan Thomas (9)	109	Tomboy	87
Sabreena Hussain	186	Tom Cabin	119
Samina Hussain	70	Tom Krause	180
Samuel Edwards	165	Tom Roach	26
Samyukta Aryasomayahjula	274	Tracey Baxter	241
Sandra Bates	134	Tracy Caller	38
Sarah Ashby	313	Tracy Green	92
Sarah Fuller	254	Troy Hodges	62
Sarah Hooper	235	Trudy Simpson	346
Sarah Louise Parry	361	T W Denis Constance	116
Sasha Lyon	270	Valerie I Hampson	24
Sharon Adkins	283	Valerie Sutton	198
Sharon Spencer	271	Valma June Streatfield	150
Sheena Blackhall	48	Verica Peacock	44
Shelley Fairclough	369	Violet M Corlett	159
Shirley Franklin	381	Y Blake	40
Shirley Perkins	45	Zoe Fitzjohn	167
Simone Mansell Broome	401	Zoë Thompson	243

Dedicated to my four wonderful Grandchildren, Jessica, Georgina, Shaun & Erin with a special thank you to Jess' who inspired me to write my poem on page 24.

The Poems
Christmas 2006

 1st January

A Little Girl And Her Shoes

For sunny days
I've sandals
with flowers on the toes.
I think one is a daisy,
and the other is a rose.

For chilly days
I've pink boots
with fur around the top
and four big, fluffy pom-poms
that go ker-flip, ker-flop.

For stormy days
I've wellingtons
to walk out in the rain
and jump in lots of puddles -
then jump in them again.

But when it's dark
and time for bed
the slippers on my feet
have rows of twinkling fairy lights
so I *dance* instead of *sleep!*

Penny Smith

2nd January

The Snowman

There he stands a figure of white
All alone in the dead of night.
A carrot nose and eyes black as coal
He really looks a friendly soul.
We'd built this snowman with such care
And the children gave him a scarf to wear.
The hours ticked by and now it was morning
Out of the window the snow is still falling.
The children can't wait to see him again
Press their little noses against the windowpane.
Out into the garden the children ran
To say hello to their special snowman,
But later that day the sun came out
Now the snowman's future was in doubt.
Little by little he melted away
For the children it was a very sad day.
Tears rolled down their cheeks, they did not laugh
As one child held a carrot, the other a scarf.

Hazell Dennison

3rd January

The Silent World Of Night

The silent world of night
The still breeze and the cool brow of white
A secret world of stillness of castles in the sky
And knights in shining armour riding high
Full moons and witches on brooms
And figures in black that go bang in the night
The silent world of night
The coldness of fright
A secret world of cats, foxes and badgers
And bats that bite
Graveyards that are silent with shadowy figures
And echoing screams that are only dreams.

Lee Allen

4th January

Pink

Pink is my favourite
In the middle of the day
Red is what it's like
When I'm going out to play

Yellow is for lunch
And orange is for tea
Purple is for when I'm tired
And sitting on your knee

Blue is for when
I don't want to finish yet
Green is for people
The kind I have just met

But pink is when I'm happiest
And everything is small
Pink is when I'm thinking
Of nothing much at all

Eileen McTeir

5th January

The Sad Bed

My bed cried again
Last night
I don't know why it stays so sad!

I leave it bread and jam
At night
For just in case it
Gets a big fright!

My friends just think my bed is bad
But I know better
My bed is sad!

Even bread and jam
At night
Doesn't help
When it gets a big fright
At night!

I leave it my toy
I leave it my teddy
But my mom says
My bed will stop crying
Right when it's ready.

Deirdre Lubbe

6th January

Bedtime Story For Isabelle

(Aged 4)

Have you heard of the fairy maiden
Who lives by the ocean blue
With hair so white that it shines at night
And whose face looks just like you.

She lived in a house in a magic land
Where the trees were brightest red
And she spoke of a strange, mysterious mouse
Which would talk to her in bed.

'It is fine,' said the mouse, 'to dance a jig.
It is fine to sing a song.
If the steps you take are not too big,
And the notes are not too wrong.'

And the fairy girl at once replied
With a wisdom and grace,
'If the song were right, we could dance all night
And end up in a different place.'

So the mouse sang sweet and tapped its feet,
And the fairy girl sang sweeter.
Then they danced away to another day
And the morning came to meet her.

Richard Stead

7th January

Questions

Why is the sky blue, not yellow or green?
Why isn't it silver? What does it mean?
Why does a rainbow bend in the middle?
Why isn't it straight? It's a bit of a riddle.

Why does lightning fork down from the sky?
Why not up from the ground? Any reason why?
Where does a flame go when you blow it out?
Does it reappear when no one's about?

They say the moon moves the tides of a great ocean sea.
Does anybody know why it doesn't move me?
Why are my feet fixed firmly to the ground?
How can I stand here and move freely around?

There are people below us on the Earth's lower face.
Why don't they fall off and drift into space?
The stars move across the night sky. This you can see.
Yet the North Star stands fixed. How can this be?

Why is the moon in such a different place every night?
Sometimes it's orange. Can this be right?
How does a caterpillar become a butterfly?
We couldn't do it, however hard we try.

Where do the winds come from? Where do they go?
Why is snow white? Does anyone know?
How do clouds float in the sky?
How are they born? How do they die?

The top of a mountain is much nearer the sun.
Yet ice and snow cover the top. Tell me, how is this done?
Does our astral spirit escape its bodily prison whilst we sleep at night?
Are our dreams its experiences till recalled at first light?

David Brown

Aunt Agatha's Garden

Dear Aunt Agatha's garden,
Is the strangest place to see.
I caught a glimpse one afternoon,
When I went round for tea.

The grass was made of spaghetti,
Overhung by broccoli trees.
Edged by rich tea fingers,
It would make you weak at the knees.

The fountain cascaded rice pudding,
While the summerhouse was of fondant and cream.
With gingerbread paths meandering,
Beside a custard stream.

The gazebo was made of bourbons,
Where sugar twists abound.
While the pond was filled with large peardrops,
At 75p for the pound.

The pool was made of nougat,
The water mocha cream.
In fact it was the sort of place,
Where you could sit and dream.

The family are often invited,
And are welcome one and all.
But if you think the garden is strange,
You should see what she's got in the hall.

Glenda Evison

 9th January

Pet Frog

'You can't have a dog, or a cat,' I was told,
So I sulked and I hid, and I cried in the cold.
It was raining outside, and the garden was wet,
But I didn't care, I just wanted a pet!

Then down by my feet something moved in the grass,
I saw something shiny, but it jumped so fast.
I had found a tiny frog, lost and sad,
(To keep it as a pet, would it really be that bad?)

I found him crouched behind a flower pot,
I scooped him up, and he seemed to breathe a lot.
His eyes were huge, and his skin was brown and green,
(If I kept him in a secret box, would it really be that mean?)

But I began to shiver as the rain beat on my coat,
And little frog looked doleful, as a croak came from his throat.
Was it fair to capture him, and keep him for myself?
He would have to be a secret, in a box, upon the shelf.

But he would cry, and maybe die, because the house was hot . . .
So I put him down, and with a frown, decided - maybe not.

Diane Bowen

10th January

Trapper Snack – The Trapdoor Spider

All the time he's building doors - it's really an obsession -
with hinges, knobs and handles, and bells for you to press on.
every key's a perfect fit and makes a great impression.

Ebony, mahogany, oak and beech and pine;
never ever shutting up till way past closing time.

Doors, doors, doors! Making more and more!
secret ones around the walls, or hidden in the floor.
He bangs them and he clips them;
he hangs them and he fits them;
he's even known to knit them
though goodness knows what for!

Out-doors and in-doors, fat doors and thin doors;
front doors and back doors, ones with wings - like jackdaws!
side-doors and trapdoors, hatch-doors and flap-doors;
never time to make pause - only time to make more doors!

Ebony, mahogany, oak and beech and pine;
never ever shutting up till way past closing time.

Every day he opens up and starts again once more,
one thought a-hammering in his head: *How I adore a door!*
He cuts and he skims them; he paints and he trims them,
he stores and he saves some; he carves and engraves some.

Busy, busy all the while, the best in all the land;
the only time he stops to eat is when a door gets jammed!

E M Caiger Gray

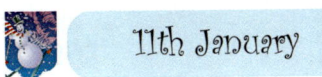 11th January

Sad Sam

It was in a strange and distant land, where some monkeys sang with a motley band;
A parrot pulled on a string or two on an old violin, painted a vivid blue.
The drummer of this strange affair was a big baboon with bright green hair;
With a flash of teeth, and a hungry grin, a crocodile banged on an old dustbin;
There was a tiger strumming on the base guitar, while a tall giraffe plucked an old sitar;
Whilst shaking the tail of a rattlesnake, Miss Mongoose chews on a fresh nut cake
They all played on quite unaware, until one day, on safari there,
An agent on his holidays, trying hard to find new ways
To introduce new stars to fame, heard this band and did exclaim;
'My goodness. What is this I hear?' Then sat a while and lent an ear.

'Something novel! Something great! This I am sure will mark my fate.
Everyone now must agree, that Sad Sam will always be,
The agent who brings back the best. A man in whom one can invest.'
So Sam approached this motley band, and holding out a friendly hand,
Walked up to the nearest there, speaking with a nonchalant air,
Said, 'Hey I'm Sad Sam, the agent who can get a lot of work for you.'
The singing stopped, the music too. Sam had caused a hullabaloo;
Monkeys leapt into the trees, to join their audience counting fleas;
The parrot dropped his violin, his squawking adding to the din;
The big baboon with his bright green hair, just stood with drumsticks in mid-air.

The bass guitarist growled and then paced around and growled again;
While Miss Mongoose leapt with such a shake she up and killed the rattlesnake;
Trying to save his instrument, the giraffe was in a predicament
With his legs all tangled in a bush, he squashed his sitar in the crush;
All that was left was the crocodile, who greeted Sam with a great big smile,
Holding on to his hand real tight . . . said, 'Can I help you with your diet?'

And . . . 'What a pity you're so thin.' Then the crocodile gave another grin . . .
Sad Sam was never seen again, he had disappeared whilst hunting fame.
Maybe he found it, maybe not. Only Mr Crocodile knows the lot.

Eileen Bailey

12th January

Gary The Glue Lover

Gary the glue lover
Is very stuck up
He pours glue on his dinner
And glue in his cup

He sticks to his pet
Who's a friendly old goat
When he swallows his food
It gets stuck in his throat

He sticks to the door
When he wants to walk through
He's a guy full of
Ickety, stickety glue

He sticks to his friends
Who are Jamie and Luke
And talks to them both
In gluegobbledegook

He sticks to the bath
When he's having a soak
This tactiley, tackety
'Tachable bloke

He got stuck up the chimney
One Christmas Eve
And was rescued by Santa
Who gave him a heave

But the worst thing that happened
To Gary with glue
Was when he got stuck
In his girlfriend's loo

Gary the glue lover
Met a sticky end
And was last seen disappearing
Through the loo's U-bend!

Valerie I Hampson

In My Bedroom

In my room with all my toys,
I like to make a lot of noise.
I also like to make a mess,
While wearing my pink princess dress.
My Barbie dolls come out to play,
Until I'm bored and then they stay
On the floor with other things,
Like a rag doll and a bear that sings.
Out comes the Playdoh and the paint,
I paint lots of pictures - all are great.
When all my toys are out on the floor,
When I am unable to find one toy more,
I go downstairs to see my mum
After having lots and lots of fun!

Karen Beedon

14th January

Us Kids

Don't them grown-ups always seem to moan.
My mum and dad are always on the phone.
Don't do this and don't do that,
It's not my fault I trod on the cat.
I didn't know stones smashed glass,
I never meant to make Dad brake so hard and give us whiplash.
He shouted at me till his veins nearly popped out,
Just when I thought it was over he even gave me a clout.
They treat me like a child but I'm seven now and a big boy.
I know me mobile phone is not a toy,
But when I put it in the sink to wash it,
Me dad only goes and has another fit.
It's not fair being little, everyone thinks you're dumb,
I don't know why, there is nothing wrong with sucking your thumb.
I know there are no Milky Ways in the galaxy
As they are two different bars,
I swear some of the things they tell you, they must think
Us kids are from Mars.
Me dad said why don't I get a paper round.
So I did, cut it into a circle, but he meant for me to walk around.
I mean I'm only a kid, what if I get lost?
What if I lose all the papers and have to pay the cost?
Me dad said he was down the mine when he was ten years old.
I told him I wouldn't have done that as it would have been cold.
I don't think me mum and dad were ever kids like us,
They had it easy, they never even had the bus,
Going everywhere in a horse and cart,
I mean what would you do if you couldn't get the horse to start?
I have the pressures of Nintendo and MP3s.
He was lucky, at sixteen he was overseas
Playing soldiers in a war I think, with his gun,
Now that is what I call a load of fun.
I could do that when I finish me tea,
But I will have to finish me new computer game,
So we will wait and see.

Tom Roach

15th January

Fish And Clips

The paper clip was dancing
I saw it, yes it's true.
It danced along the shelf where sat
A bottle that was blue.
And inside that blue bottle
A sign flashed, 'Make a Wish',
I did and guess what happened,
I got a red goldfish.
Now I didn't want a goldfish,
Especially one in red,
I hid my disappointment
And took the paper clip instead.
This made the clip quite angry
And it let out a loud cry.
It screamed and screamed for ages
Then it saw the fish swim by.
'Hey Fishy, help,' it shouted.
And the fish stopped swimming round.
'Yo, Clippy, what you doing?
Tell that loon to put you down.'
Well I was just astounded,
Gobsmacked some would say.
I dropped Clippy in with Fishy
And quickly moved away.

Liz Cozens

In Trouble

I got in trouble yesterday for bouncing on my bed,
It made me awfully out of breath and turned my face all red,
My daddy told me, 'Listen hard, I'd rather you were sat
With a quiet book upon your lap, don't bounce around like that.'
But I was too busy having fun to listen to what he said,
Until I slipped upon the sheet and fell and bumped my head!

Polly Cordell

17th January

Bad Night

Running down the corridors
were young and fearsome dinosaurs.
Their skin looked wet and greeny-brown,
one glared at me with gruesome frown.
It swished its tail and had bad breath,
I was really scared to death.
I saw its teeth and dripping jaws
and ran through one of the large doors.
I slammed the door in frightened state,
because I thought I might be ate.
Yes, hot dinner for T-rex young
if this flimsy door was sprung.
A cupboard door opened in haste,
T-rex had come to have a taste.
I felt its breath upon my head
and didn't move, I acted dead.
The seconds felt like hours for me
as T-rex sniffed repeatedly.
All of a sudden he was gone,
my heart pulsated on and on.
I heard a miaow in my ear,
my cat had taken all my fear
and made the bad dream go away,
so I could live another day.

Linda Knight

18th January

The Creature!

Long ago, in a forest deep
Lived a creature that did not sleep.
It lurked, it stalked
it cringed, it walked
but most of all it did creep!

The creature had an ugly face
with warts and spots all over the place.
They bubbled and blurted
and oozed and they spurted
he really was a terrible case!

The creature's mouth was long and droolish,
the creature's brain was dumb and foolish.
His eyes they were sad
and his body was bad
but he was actually cool-ish!

For despite his looks, you shall see
he filled up people's hearts with glee
and made people feel lovely
although he was ugly
and how do I know? He is me!

There's a lesson right here, you listen fully
never be mean and never to bully,
be friendly to others
like sisters and brothers
and life will be warm, nice and woolly.

Karl Mercer

19th January

The Pirate's Hornpipe

(For Ruth)

The night-time shadow hid its wake
As sleepy hollow swings a gate.
A silver cloud hugged the sail
Behind the stars, they leave no trail.

It's the pirate ship of Black-Eyed Jim,
The mottled crew with Scurvy Tim.
They plague the sky with wicked intent
Once leaving a spaceship with a dent!

The aim of pirates is 'steal what they can'
But this Jolly Roger has another plan!
Black-Eyed Jim and his scallywag crew
Seek out naughty children - where? Only they knew.

In the night when children's dreams are a-flight
A blackened ship comes ashore for a fright!
For children who are mean to all
These pirates from shadow to door come to call.

From other tales, to you it may seem
That all pirates are dirty, nasty and mean
(and you be right!)
For after their antics of scaring them brats
They return to their decks and drink rum from their hats.

Then, as they flitter behind the moon
They dance to the hornpipe and shout,
'We'll be back soon!'

Kim Taylor

20th January

Bruss The Dog

Bruss ran down the lane with his nose in the air
Every so often he would stand and stare
He was looking for something, goodness knows what
He wasn't telling, so maybe he forgot

He stopped when he came to a clump of weeds
And cocked his leg over them and instantly peed
Then smelt what he did and continued to run
On his way, tongue hanging out, looking for fun

Just then he saw from the corner of one eye
A big joint of meat that the butcher left by
The back door, for the woman in one-ninety-three
Bruss grabbed it quick and took it home for his tea

Bruss ate the joint then chewed at the bone
The theft was discovered, but the thief was unknown
But Bruss was not bothered, who cares if he ate
The woman's meat joint, that was just fate

Bruss gave it no thought as he slept by the fire
Dreaming of butchers with meat on the wire
Just hanging there, for him to seize
A string of sausages, he did it often with ease

One day Bruss bit off more than he could chew
He was caught by the butcher stealing a spare rib or two
He instinctively put on a forlorn expression
Hung his head in shame, waiting for pardon of his transgression

It worked, and in fact he was not only set free
But given a bone by the butcher to take home for his tea
This is the life, thought Bruss as he ran down the lane
He's quite nice is that butcher, I'll visit him again!

Liane Bell

21st January

My Teddy Bear

I like my darling Teddy Bear
He's soft and warm and cuddly
He makes a funny, squeaky noise
He is so sweet and lovely.

His pads and paws are in brown felt
With matching suede-tipped nose
He sleeps beside me every night
Side by side upon the pillows.

He goes for rides in dolly's pram
To town on shopping sprees
He even went to school one day
Has pride of place at party teas.

He's not as new as once he was
His coat in places worn
But still I love him just the same
As when he was first born.

Elizabeth Love

22nd January

The Tooth Fairy

Hiding behind the curtain
in the corner of the room
waiting there ready to pounce
in the ever-increasing gloom
biding his time
till you've closed your eyes
so he's sure that you're asleep
then, employing all his cunning
out of his corner he will creep
across the floor and round the bed
till he can see your face
he'll slip his hand under your pillow
take your tooth
and put money in its place
but if you try to catch him
he'll take your tooth away
and you won't find any money
when you awake next day.

Daphne Cornell

23rd January

Mischievous Fleas

Two little fleas were playing in a rug,
Planning who was next in line for them to vex and bug,
After careful thinking over a chit-chat,
They decided on a raid on the family cat.
So, knowing all the tricks that are common to the flea,
Attacked the cat mischievously and jumped around with glee.
But the cat was wise to them and with one big, hefty pat,
Threw the fleas at flying speed back to their home, the mat.

Laura Clarke

24th January

The Tragic Fate Of Bouncy Boy

Freddie did bounce, for bouncing was fun;
No greater joy lived that he thought could be done.
He'd bounce on his bed and then on the floor,
Kangaroo-hopping through many a door.
But 'twas a trifle unpleasant to family and friends;
His hopping, it seemed, had no clear end,
Nor beginning, nor middle, if truth be known . . .
Throughout his short life his habit just grown.
And so fierce was the pounding upon the oak floor,
That from his frail feet blood freely did pour.
So the softest of surfaces Freddie would seek,
Until his bed-bouncing met a horrible peak
When the soft bed mattress gave swiftly away,
And there in sheer agony he silently lay.
For Freddie had found that bouncing has risks;
For him it involved several slipped discs.
And bleeding now not from his feet but his head -
But not bad enough that he'd quite end up dead -
A lesson was all that from it he read:
One cannot bounce safely, even 'pon one's own bed.

David Maidment

25th January

Imagination

There's a place called imagination
Where anyone can go
Just follow the path inside your mind
Great places then you will find
Green velvet carpets become forests and lands
Sparkling trees with leaves of diamonds
Rivers and lakes, shimmering silver and gold
Flowing to the underworld, to a sea below
There in splendour sits a king, on majestic throne
Playing his harp to mermaids that sing
With voices tinkling of angels' tone
Then Neptune takes you by the hand
To another wonderland
There, inside a shimmering cave
Lined with pearls that oysters made
O, the magic of the deep
Shipwrecks lay forever asleep
Untouched inside a treasure trove
Caskets filled with coins of gold
In this place called imagination
Anyone can go
Have an adventure, take a journey
To the great unknown!

Patricia Johnson

26th January

Funny Feet

At the end of our legs
Grow two things lumpy and odd
Yet without them we'd fall over
And not run, walk or plod!

They come in all shapes and sizes
Hairy, bony, small and big
They could be hooves on a horse
Or trotters on a pig!

Sometimes smelly or full of sock fluff
Or with toes painted nice and neat
There's nothing sillier, nothing stranger
Than the sight of our bare feet!

With five toes short and stumpy
Like a disfigured hand
A heel round as a snooker ball
And bits that always catch the sand!

Fat people cannot reach them
Babies suck on them in bed
And acrobats, weirdest of all
Choose to walk on hands instead!

You can dance on them and swim with them
Make footprints in the snow
A ballerina stands up straight and tall
On just a single toe!

They may look a bit freaky
But they move us as far as we choose
But however much we love our feet
They're best tucked away in shoes!

Tracy Caller

27th January

The Wedding

Fitzgerald was a handsome frog
He had a bright green coat
The shoes were red upon his feet
He wore a bow tie at his throat

He owned the biggest lily pad
His walking stick was smart
He loved the princess of the frogs
She had given him her heart

They planned a wedding oh so posh
With Freddie on the flute
Jimmy on the fiddle
In his brand new wedding suit

There was Faye upon the organ
Bill played the drums so grand
Vera on the saxophone
Oh! what a lovely band

The minister was Frankfurt
From another lily pad
The locals said the wedding
Was the best they'd ever had

The honeymoon was wonderful
Spent on another stream
In a hotel called 'The Tadpole'
Beneath a full moonbeam.

Joyce Newton

28th January

There's A Hole In Your Hair

There's a hole in your hair Grandpa,
I saw it last night,
When you bent down to kiss me,
And Mary, goodnight.
But never mind Grandpa;
You're still as fit as can be.
You can still run, and jump,
Like all my friends and me.

And I'll tell you what Grandpa,
I'll get some of Mummy's grey wool
And patch up that hole,
Until it's quite full.

Y Blake

29th January

Big Kids On Little Kids

I was afraid of the world when I was a child,
Disorder, mistrust and everything wild.
The cars on the road and the kids at the park.
Shadows on walls that crept in with the dark.
Invisible monsters that no one could see,
Lay under my bed to jump out on me.
Afraid to tell the truth but afraid to lie.
Not wanting to say - just wanting to cry.
But as you get older the more that you know
That life's not so scary as you continue to grow.
There aren't any monsters waiting to call,
And the shadows - reflections that dance on the wall.
The kids on the park, have kids of their own,
And the car you were afraid of is outside your home . . .
So try to be happy - don't wish life away,
You're not a child long - you'll be grown up one day.

Karen Cormick

30th January

Best Friends

I have two very special friends,
They both live in my street.
We play together every night
Though we have to be discreet.

Harry, he's the eldest,
Is black and very handy.
Cyril has a gammy leg
And a weakness for cough candy.

I brought them home a week ago,
To meet my mum and dad,
But Mum just screamed and went all green
And Dad was just as bad!

I tried to say how good they were.
I said, 'Just keep your cool.'
Mum said, 'Get them out of here!'
And Dad jumped off his stool!

Dad said he would fetch a box,
To put my best friends in.
I said Dad could stroke one
Then they'd be friends with him.

Harry gave his biggest smile
And Cyril blew a kiss,
But Dad bashed down the rolling pin,
I prayed that he would miss!

My chums have got the message now,
They're feeling rather sad,
'Cos no one loves a *tar-an-tu-la,*
Except for this brave lad!

Sue Hansard

31st January

Early Birdie

A robin did a plan devise
On how to make an earthworm rise
From his home within the ground
Fat and juicy, plump and round

He thought he'd charm it like a snake
With a tuneful song that he'd make
Then he'd grab it in his beak
So that juicy worm couldn't make a squeak.

Well, all was fine and the earthworm rose
From his home in which he dozed
He danced and swayed to the robin's song
But all at once his plan went wrong
For as the robin stopped his tune
The earthworm slid back in his home
For the trance would cease when the music stopped
And back in the ground the earthworm popped.

Poor robin sang and sang all day
In an effort to catch his slippery prey
But in the end with nothing to eat
He had to admit defeat
The earthworm he'd had the greatest fun
Dancing all day in the summer sun
And poor old robin it is true
The earthworm made a cuckoo of you.

D E Cornell

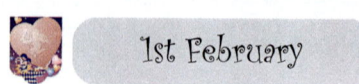 1st February

The Rabbit And The Snail

A rabbit met a snail
on his way to school.
'Why are you so lazy?' he asked.
'I'm not as a rule,'
replied the poor snail.
'If you had to drag
your house on your back
you would be slowed down
and you could not fast track.'

The rabbit thought it over
decided the snail was right,
they made up and became friends -
together strolled out of sight!

Verica Peacock

2nd February

Gobblydegook

Gobblydegook the cat is squishy and fat
as he pads on the carpet, his eyes spy a rat

The rat is lean and quick on his toes
while the cumbersome cat is striking a pose

Too late, the moggie is flat on his back
as the rat weaves past him and slips through a crack

But all is not lost as the cat uses cunning
he uses his paws instead of running

And swiftly he scoops the rat up in glee
and savours the thought of Ratty for tea!

Shirley Perkins

3rd February

Amanda Who?

Amanda is just five years old
You would not know unless you were told
A chatterbox, her speech so gay
Will send you happy on your way.
Away to school she waves goodbye
Leaving you without a sigh.
A day to paint that smiling face
On any cloud the day may grace,
Returning home at half-past three
Chatting gaily, wants her tea.
Bringing smiles back home to me,
Amanda, may you always be
Happy, carefree, along life's way.

Pamela Gormley

4th February

Muck Magnet

He sat upon the doorstep, then rolled across the lawn,
George's brother were at school, he felt lonely and forlorn.
He had no one else to play with, only their old dog,
Mam and him could go to the woods and maybe find a frog.
But he wouldn't kiss it like those soppy girls,
He'd keep it under his pillow, to see if his hair would curl.

He ate his lunch upon the wall, then sat upon the bin,
He poked his tongue out when next-door's baby stared at him.
He rode his trike along the path and found an ant or two.
He put them in his pocket, cos he wanted to start a zoo.
He climbed onto the shed roof and sang a rainbow song,
When would his brothers come home? He hoped it wouldn't be long.

He picked some nettles and some daisies, a bunch of flowers for Mam,
Then ate a sticky sandwich, his favourite, blackberry jam.
The jam dripped down his shirt front and down his trousers too,
Mixing with the mud on them, making a tasty goo.
He had 'marto sauce in his hair and snot upon his sleeve,
Just how much dust ran from nose to toes, you never would believe!

When at last he came inside to watch a bit of TV,
Drastic measures were called for, that much Mam could plainly see.
She chased him round the table, the sofa and even the chair,
Before she snatched him in her arms and took him up the stairs.
She plopped him in the bathtub full of water and suds,
She washed him quickly and between his toes she used cotton buds.

Soon he was clean and dry, then wrapped in a blanket, snug,
He dozed off to sleep, dreaming of being a bug . . .

Helen Smith

5th February

Ellen Knight

Ellen Knight from Tunbridge Wells
Thought she'd try her hand at spells
Found inside a witch's book
By a froggy, soggy brook.

First, she turned her sister's braces
Into caterpillar's laces
Next, to vex her brother Eddy
Her magic powers shrank his teddy
Which fell down in the toilet bowl
One flush and it was swallowed whole.

Her ma said, 'Ellen, eat your greens.'
She changed them into fairy queens
Which flew ten times around the telly
Frightening to fits, her Aunty Nelly.

When Pa grew cross and tried to shout
Her magic whisked his dentures out
They jumped across the room and flew
Into her granny's Irish stew
And there they sank beneath the gravy
Like two old dinghies from the navy.

Grown bold, she changed her cousin's cat
Into a tiger large and fat
Which went with her to the theatre
And at the curtain fall, it ate her.

So, little girls who'd like to be
A witch of power and mystery
Make dog or mouse or fish go splat
But never *ever* change a cat!

Sheena Blackhall

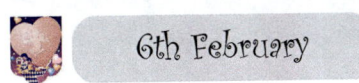

6th February

When I Grow Up I Want To . . .

When I'm bigger and all grown up
I won't read a newspaper,
or drink coffee from a cup.

I don't see why grown-ups groan all the time,
they should be called groan-ups,
because all they do is whine.

I'm stressed they reply when asked how are you?
I think this is a groan-up invention,
otherwise kids would be stressed too.

It seems to have been invented because they go to work,
work sends their brains barmy,
and makes groan-ups berserk.

When I grow up I'm not going to get a real job,
don't worry about me though,
I won't be short of a few bob.

I'm going to become an inventor of great inventory things,
like a self-hovering Hoover
and a washing machine which sings.

Life will be great when I get big,
because I'll stay exactly the same,
but I'll just be a bigger kid!

Rebecca Guest

7th February

The Snurgle

The snurgle
lives down the plughole.
He's as quiet as quiet can be.
All day he sits in the S-bend,
in the dark, so he can't see.

The snurgle
hides from all people,
because he's ever so shy.
He lives off hair and toenails,
and he squirts soap in your eye.

The snurgle
can't speak as we can.
He can only make one sound,
and that's the snurgling gurgle
you hear when the bath's running down.

The snurgle
drinks all of the water.
Though he's small, he's very long.
He loves the scum and the bubbles,
and his breath really does pong.

The snurgle
is scared of all humans.
Keeps well away, out of our reach,
and slithers away down the S-bend,
if ever he smells any bleach.

So next time you hear that snurgle
as the bath water's running down,
don't worry that you might have killed him,
for now you know snurgles can't drown.

Harry Lyons

7th February

8th February

Unicorn Union

One dark early morn, I awoke from a sound,
That rose up through my window, though it came from the ground.
I ran to the window, and there I did see,
A pure white unicorn, gazing right up at me!

It chewed on a clump of our garden's heather,
Then it spoke in the softest angelic voice ever.
'Come, little Brad, let's go for a ride,
While the menfolk are sleeping still, our secret will hide.'
So, without delay, I ran out to greet,
This magical creature which stood at my feet.
'My name is Sasha, and I heard your prayers,
But the angels are dealing with those adult affairs.
For now, do not worry about worldly concern,
Be a child now, and enjoy what children can learn.
I know that you worry about starvation and war,
But the angels will deal with these menfolk, I'm sure.
Hop onto my back, and I'll take you to lands,
With crystal-blue waters, and shimmering gold sands.'
Without delay, I mounted her back,
And we galloped away from Earth's beaten track.
We travelled so fast, time and space were no more,
Till we came to a halt on a faraway shore.
We splashed in the sea, wrote our names in the sand,
Hers was written by hoof prints, mine with my hand.
We basked in the warmth of the sun from above,
I stroked her white mane, and my heart filled with love.
'I can see now, sweet unicorn, life's not all that bad,
That I don't have to always feel angry or sad.
Your love is enough to warm my sore heart,
And I'll now feel your love, even when we're apart.'
Reassuring, her velvety nose nudged my hand,
Then it's time now, to return to mankind's land.
Close your eyes and imagine you are back in your bed,
With your feathered pillow nestled, under your head.'

8th February

I did this, then slowly opened my eyes,
Squinting up at the window, and the morning sunrise.
i thought, *was my unicorn ride just a dream?*
What was its purpose, what did it mean?
I ran to the window, looked for clues,
And sure enough, in the heather, were prints of horseshoes.
'Oh my!' as I looked at my bedclothes with glee,
They were salty and sandy, still damp from the sea!
'Oh my!' It was real. I now understand,
That unicorns and angels, can give a helping hand.
As long as we ask for their help, they'll appear,
To assist us, and guide us, through worry and fear.
So when you get hunches, or thoughts cross your mind,
Know it's a message from the angel or unicorn kind!

Martina Radford

9th February

Annie The Artist Went To The Zoo

Annie the artist went to the zoo.
She took pots of paint with her,
ten brushes too.

She painted an elephant bright emerald-green -
the lion cub purple, a sight to be seen.

The crocodile violet? A strange looking fellow
and would you believe she made the monkeys yellow?

The tiger turned crimson, its tail a brilliant hue -
and the puma turned pink on Annie's day at the zoo.

Six squiggles she slapped on a horse and a yak,
turquoise and black from the front to the back.

Annie splished and she sploshed all over the deer
and coated with orange a grizzly old bear.

Ducklings swam past as blue as the sky.
'Red spots would be better,' she said with a sigh.

Three hippopotami stood by the gate.
Annie looked at her watch and said,
'Sorry, I'm late.'

She picked up her paints,
waved farewell to the zoo,
the gate now was gleaming -
it was red, white and blue . . .

Annie the artist had painted that too!

Paula Slack

10th February

What's In A Name?

Come along *Tail-End Chuck*
It's time for us to go
Put your boots on, grab your hat
Let's get out in the snow

That's the way, *Clever Clogs*
You're doing very well
You threw that snowball oh so hard
How far away it fell

Hold on tight *Cuddle-Chops*
We're going down so fast
Racing all the other kids
Let's hope that we're not last

Oops-a-daisy *Silly-Bill*
That bit's really slippy
See the way that giant drift
Looks like a Mr Whippy

Clap-a-handies *Jumpy-Jim*
That was really fun
And now to stop us getting cold
Back home again we'll run

Safe and warm now *Sweetie-Pie*
And now time for a treat
What's that you say? You'd really like . . .
A sweetie pie to eat?

Linda Howitt

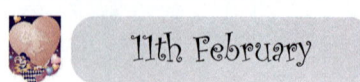 11th February

Sweetest Of Dreams

I wrote the sweetest of dreams for you,
It's for you alone to keep
And I hope you will remember it
Every time you go to sleep.

So dream of a land
Where sherbet is sand
And trees are candyfloss,
With liquorice roads
And pink bubblegum toads
That all swim in a cherryade foss.

Then dream of a place
Where sugar mice race
To get to the chocolate cheese,
And everywhere, you can taste the air
Which blows in on a peppermint breeze.

Then dream of a world
Where caramel grass is unfurled
To show butterscotch underneath,
With lollipop signs
And toffee from mines
That never rot your teeth.

Michael Campbell

12th February

Just A Bug

I am just a bug
And I like to have some fun
It happens mostly in your garden
When your daily work is done
I look around your plants
They are in lines and oh so neat
Then I decide which one's the best
That's the first one I will eat

Next it's to the greenhouse
You win prizes by the score
If I take one bite from all you grow
Bet you don't win anymore
Next onto your apples
Shouldn't eat them late at night
So I think I'll spoil a few
By just taking one large bite

Now it's time for me to go
To the garden right next door
He also grows prize plants
And I've not been here before
But Friday night's the best
I will meet up with my mates
Then we eat up all the plants
They grow at number twenty-eight

P M Stone

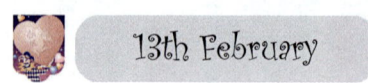 13th February

I Know A Secret

I know a secret.
I know who moves your favourite toy and who makes the socks odd.
I know who makes the mess with the cereal in the kitchen and the toys in the bedroom.
They live at the bottom of the garden amongst the birds and bugs.
They love sweets and sugary treats and fruit of all kinds.
So when you see a flash of colour fly by, it's not a butterfly, no,
Maybe it was one of the fairies that live at the bottom of your garden.
So think twice when a sock is made odd or your favourite toy goes missing.
Maybe it was not Mummy or Daddy; maybe it was the fairies playing a game,
But shush, don't tell, it's our little secret.

Paul Green

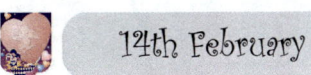

14th February

Slug

My name is Slug and as you can see
I may not be pretty like a butterfly,
or be able to soar in the sky.
I slither and slide, I'm ever so slow,
But let me tell you about some friends I know . . .

Here's my friend the ladybird,
Have you heard? She's red and shiny,
with round black dots
that look like great big full stops.

And here is Worm.
Watch him wiggle, watch him squirm
through tiny gaps in the ground.
He doesn't even make a sound.

Here comes Butterfly
with her colourful wings, she flutters by.
She rests on a leaf on a warm summer's day
and watches the children in the garden play.

Bee is busy when it's sunny
collecting pollen to make her honey.
Buzz, buzz, buzz, all the day through
making honey for me and you.

Michele Howe

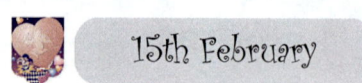
15th February

So Many Questions

The sun won't wait
On the globe's other side
While it touches there with light
On our side it's still night
Here people sleep and yawn
There a new day has dawned.

Mom, where's the other side?
Is it reversed, at slow pace?
Or far beyond our border are
Their clocks ahead in the race?

The sun won't go out
It burns very slow
So many questions, my curious child
I only wish I could know.

Mom, who turns the Earth?
Why do we cry?
Who invented such words
As 'so long' and 'goodbye'?
Is everything different, or more of the same?
Are we a toy, or some computer's game?
Why do we feel pain?
Where is the past?
Do all creatures love with their hearts?

The sun won't go out
It burns very slow
Many more questions, my curious child
And I don't really know.

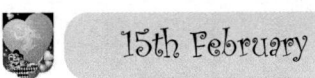 15th February

Mom, when did time start
When will it stop
Who was before us?
Who will come after?
Where are we taken
And where do we go
What is 'forever'
And where is 'below'?

The sun won't go out
It burns very slow
So many questions, my curious child
Like you, I wish I could know.

Nava Semel

16th February

Untitled

Learning is good, learning is fun
Reading and writing, or even a sum
Start with a number
Let's try number one
What can I say, what shall I do?
Let's add another
That makes two
Aha, let's see
Here's another
Now we have three
And once more
So now we have four
Then we arrive at number five
One more will fix
Our number to six
Now it's seven
That's number heaven
Can't be late
The number's at eight
Moving along, feeling fine
Numbers are rising, now it's nine
One more number, here it is then
Now I have numbers one up to ten

Troy Hodges

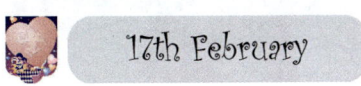

17th February

The Pirate

When I grow up I'm going to be a pirate, bad and bold
And sail the sea and rob the rich of all their precious gold.
A secret map will point the way to where I hide the treasure,
Bones, a skull and a secret code, the distance it will measure.

I'll fly the Jolly Roger from the mast of my big ship
And have a pistol in my belt, I can fire from the hip.
I'll wear a patch on one eye and have an evil grin,
With a parrot on my shoulder; my fights I'll always win.

A knife I'll carry in my teeth when I board a rival boat,
Throw scurvy knaves overboard and hope that they can float.
I'll sit upon a barrel of rum and sing out, 'Yo ho ho'
And stop at desert islands where no one else dare go.

I'll have a tattoo on my arm that says 'I love you Mother'
And when I have some time to spare I'll go and get another.
I'll sail away when people come and try to capture me,
The only time I'll come ashore is when Mummy calls out, 'Tea!'

J M Gallen

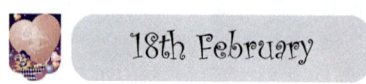

18th February

The Diddy Jibbers

You know that urge that children have, to pick and poke and jibby-jab?
Well here's a tale you should be glad that I have shared with you,
For little Molly ignored the rules and learned her lesson from a very cruel
And ghoulish trip to Diddy Jibber Land, where they eat 'chopped children stew'.

Molly was soaking in the bath when she poked her big toe up the tap,
'I've gottcha!' something cheered and clapped, then out popped an angry face.
The Diddy Jibber pulled out the plug, there was a ghastly glug glug glug,
Then 'Urp!' the plughole belched and squelched poor Molly through its grate.

'Where am I?' our young Molly cried, she drew in her breath and rubbed her eyes,
For my oh my the sight she spied was a gruesome one indeed.
It was a world of tiny toes and fingers collected by the Diddy Jibbers
And lined up like short fat caterpillars to build their grisly streets.

There were houses made of severed toes, and fields were gated with rows and rows
Of sewn together fingers and thumbs and hacked off bits of flesh.
Said the Jibber, 'We don't like boys' foul feet, they're sweaty, nasty, they pong and reek,
But girls' clean toes are quite a treat, and yours look ripe and fresh.'

Jibber Land made Molly queasy and the Jibber woman made her more uneasy
For in her hand she was wielding an axe for Molly's toes.
'When you children get the fidgets, you stick your podgy, dirty digits
Into holes you flibbertigibbets know full well to leave alone.'

Well Molly put up quite a tussle and wrestled free from the Jibber's muscle
And amidst that quite mad axe kerfuffle she saw a sudsy rope.
So up she climbed, in quite a lather, *oomphed* and groaned,
    wondered *how much farther?*
Then, hurrah, she was in her bath - and she blocked the taps with lots of soap.

So take my advice and don't pick and poke, unless you want to swirl and float
Into the crazy Dibber Jibber world of gnawed off fingers and toes.
And while we're at it I may as well warn you, just in case it hasn't dawned on you,
Please do take caution when you pick your nose . . .
    For who's to say quite where that finger might go . . .

Carly Dugmore

19th February

Be Happy As You Are

Long, long ago, when the world was slow
And the skies were always blue,
There lived a little girl - a naughty little girl
(I hope she was nothing like you).

For whatever she had, this girl who was bad,
She wanted a different thing.
If she had cake she didn't want cake,
But a piece of the pink icing.

And when she went out she would throw her weight about
And cry to be home again,
But when she was in she made such a din
To go splashing about in the rain.

If she had meat it was stuff she couldn't eat
And cried for fish instead.
She wouldn't get up, cos she hated getting up,
But she hated going to bed.

Then one day in the early part of May
She grew tired of playing with the girls.
She wished to be a boy (cos she wasn't a boy)
And cut off all her curls.

Then, my dear, she felt very queer,
Her voice became hard and coarse.
And before you could say - well, whatever you would say -
That girl had turned to a horse.

I needn't tell you this tale isn't true,
But the moral's as clear as a door:
Be happy as you are, or, whatever you are,
You'll get more than you bargained for!

Leslie Rocker

Shopping Day

The shopping trolley whizzed on wheels
Mrs Cow clicking her brown shoe heels
Swaggering her tail as groceries she picked
Knocking old Mr Chicken off his walking stick
Mrs Lamb helped him on his way
As Mrs Cow picked the pile of hay
From the shelf Pony collected grass
As Mrs Goat went trotting past
To reach for a bag of fresh carrots
Knocking out her paw by two flying parrots
Snorting two piglets entered the door
Poor Mrs Fox slid along the floor
Her full basket went flying into the air
Tripping on tins she fell onto a chair
Tom Cat serving Miss Shepherd Dog
Shouted for help from Mrs Frog
Who leapt to the counter saying next
As Mr Bull charged forward very vexed
Saying the parrots were causing fright
To Mrs Goat who had been up all night
Mrs Cow's tail had old Mr Chicken down
Causing Tom Cat to scratch and frown
The pigs were trotting their paws all dirt
Causing Mrs Fox to slip and get hurt
The parrots kept flying and flying around
Bags of white flour fell to the ground
Poor Mrs Turkey gobbled with fright
Her coat of feathers were all white
With the sound of a bell ringing outside
The two parrots started to panic and hide
In flight two eagles entered the shop
As lemonade bottles started to pop

 20th February

The eagle policemen had been ordered to
Arrest the parrots escaped from the zoo
Wisely they collected an old onion net bag
Pleased many of the animals' tails did wag
Arresting the parrots the crows flew away
Everyone thanking them for saving the day

Brian Frost

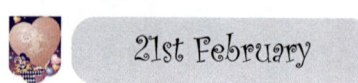 21st February

Feet

Smelly, sweaty, long things,
Stuck at the end of your legs,
If nobody wore shoes or socks,
We'd all be wearing pegs,
To block the foul, disgusting stench
Of cheesy, smelly toes,
So if someone takes their socks off,
Don't forget to block your nose!

Hayley Hopkins

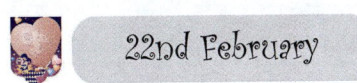 22nd February

The Family Down The Road

The family down the road are really bad and smelly
The daddy, name of Reg, has a gigantic wobbly belly
It hangs over his belt nearly down to his shoeses
So that whatever he drops he nearly always loses
The mummy, name of Rosy, smells like cabbage and she's nosy
One of the kids, name of Florrie, is always itching and scratching
So you never ever know what you might be catching
Another kid, name of Herbert has an ever-running nose
With green and yellow stuff hanging down to his toes
There's an auntie, name of Bertha, whose breath can knock you down
Best to be avoided if you see her round the town
The granny, name of Queenie, looks just like a toad
And lets off wind so loud you can hear it up the road
It's very naughty to laugh but they really are that bad
I don't think they've heard of soap, don't you think that's sad?

Elizabeth Morton

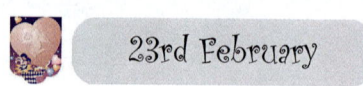
23rd February

The Pixie Of Secrets

There was a funny woman who couldn't keep a secret inside
There was no tale she didn't share, nothing she could hide
If she was told a secret her tummy grew a lot
And if she didn't say it, it would go pop!

Well one day she was spilling secrets here and there
A pixie appeared right out of nowhere
The pixie said if the woman was to keep a secret for a day or two
Anything she'd want she can have, and with that off she flew

So the woman held her tummy in tight and promised not to tell
And after each hour it slowly began to swell
It was growing bigger and bigger like a big balloon
And the funny woman was hoping it would end very soon

But time passed very slowly indeed
The only thing that kept her going was her greed!
But as she hung out the washing in the backyard
She heard a secret from over the fence, and keeping it would be very hard!

The pixie giggled away as the funny woman yelped in pain
She was so big by now that she was larger than an aeroplane
She'd blown up an' up into the sky and looked so very funny
But all she thought about was what she'd wish for . . . all that money!

The neighbours saw her and couldn't believe their eyes
'Look, look!' they shouted, 'the funny woman's in the sky'
The pixie laughed and laughed till she went red in the face
She never met anyone who blew up at such a pace.

The funny old woman soon blew up so huge and went pop
And learned too late that if you spill secrets, you really should stop!

Samina Hussain

24th February

Astral Paine

I'm zooming through the universe
At the super speed of light
The Earth is like a little pearl
Surrounded by the night.
I'm captain of a spaceship
That's called the Argonaut
My name is Astral Paine
And I'm an astronaut.

Four of us make up the crew
Ricky, Dan, then Doc and me
We work together in a team
Weightless – as in micro-gravity.
At night we sleep in zipped-up cots
Tiny cabins of just two berth
We move around by push and pull
There's nothing like it down on Earth.

Yes! we're on a special mission
First stop, we land on Mars
And I'm off collecting samples
To take back home in jars.
Then we're going on to Jupiter
The biggest planet in the sky
It has a mini solar system
And four moons or satellites.

Our shuttle is like a tin can
It grumbles and it creaks
Last night we felt the meteorites
And now the shuttle leaks.
It means we're coming home again
Much sooner than I'd thought
And first I'm gonna have a bath -
Put on the telly - and watch the sport.

Di Mundell

Child's Play

There is a place, not far away,
Where gnomes and pixies love to play.
Where trees are made of marzipan
Which if you want to eat, you can.

The lakes are full of lemonade,
And fairies dance within the shade
Of bushes full of cherry drops
And aniseed and Coco Pops.

Marshmallow clouds adorn a sky
Where elephants just love to fly
Above a meadow, made of jam,
Where stands an icing sugar lamb.

Honey vines grow straight and tall,
Their sugared catkins ripe to fall
Upon the grass, which tastes of lime,
Or orange in the wintertime!

Syrup bushes hide small elves,
Who, naturally, just help themselves
To all the jellies they can see
In raspberry and custard trees.

There is a place, not far away,
Where you may go some summer's day.
Where trees are made of marzipan
Which is you want to eat, you can!

Anne Rolfe-Brooker

26th February

Tick-Tock, Bedroom Clock

Tick-tock,
Bedroom clock
Waken me on a day
Of pealing bells
And magic spells
And laughter at all that I say.

If I cry help the tears to dry
And my day will be full of you.

Tick-tock,
Bedroom clock
Till sleep quietens you,
Faces and places
May leave their traces
But embraces make it all true.

Take the time to tickle me pink
And I'll give all my love to you.

Pip Hill

27th February

Little Blackie

Within my weekends,
away from school,
I would dance through fields,
nearby - so cool,
until one day - out of the blue,
a puppy appeared,
as black as a shoe.

Where did you descend from,
my little black lamb?
You must be lost - surely,
my name is Sam,
we danced and played,
for many long hours,
myself and little Blackie,
jumping over the flowers.

Each weekend I spent,
playing among the grass,
little Blackie appeared,
so bold as brass,
I'll call you Blackie,
for you're so divine,
he gave a glad woof,
so now he is mine.

Steve Kettlewell

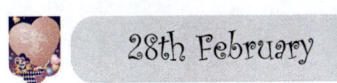

28th February

Mokey The Lazy Donkey

He was a lazy donkey,
Who wouldn't move an inch,
I pulled him and I pushed him,
But he didn't even flinch.

For he just stood and laughed at me,
Hee! Haw! Hee! Haw! He said,
You'll never make me move from here,
I simply won't be led.

Then I had a brilliant notion,
I found a piece of stick,
Attacked it to a carrot,
With string, that did the trick.

I dangled it in front of him,
Hee! Haw! Hee! Haw! He said,
Now that's a juicy offering,
As up the road we fled!

Now Mokey was a silly ass!
He was a stupid Ned!
He thought that he could laugh at me,
But I hee-hawed instead!

Annie McKimmie

1st March

Howard

Howard, from the minute he was born howling
And growing up continued scowling
Lying in his cot as a tiny babe
Screaming so much, making his mother a slave
Demanding to be carried all through the night
Lack of sleep left parents very uptight!
During the toddler stage nothing much improved
He carried on in the same old groove
Tantrums, tears and screams galore
Lots of kicking and drumming his feet on the floor
His parents were really at their wits' end
Who could they ask - for whom could they send?
The day finally dawned when Howard started school
Miss was experienced and nobody's fool
When Howard started screaming he was promptly taken away
He sat isolated for the rest of the day
While the class all enjoyed playing triangles and drums
Howard felt lonely and missed all the fun
It didn't end there though, Howard still didn't learn
Next day he's lying down on the floor
Not willing to get up so he's shown the door
Lonesome and crying, his tears wouldn't stop
But still the penny wouldn't drop!
However, dawned the glorious day
When Howard chose not to have his way
Fed up with missing all the good things
Feeling like an angel who wants his wings
When he felt like giving someone a whack
The lonely scene stopped him in his tracks
He began to share things and stayed calm
Knowing this behaviour would do him no harm
Miss smiled and sensed she had won
Now Howard could always join in the fun
His parents were very relieved of course
No more shouting themselves hoarse
Instead of an offspring, obnoxious and wild
Howard is a calm, polite and friendly child.

Annette Griffiths

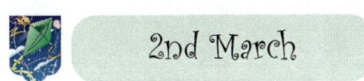

2nd March

Recipe For A Monster

(Be prepared to run when the recipe's finished)

Dragon paws,
Demon claws,
Mix and stir with fear.
Monkey tails,
Lizard scales,
Throw in a lion's ear.
Shake the mix,
Add pixie tricks,
Or maybe a fairy's tear.
Then add some weeds,
An ogre's tweeds,
Completion's almost near.
So finish off,
With pickled sloth . . .
And then get out of here!

Jay Berkowitz

3rd March

Pussycat, Pussycat, Where Have You Been?

The dowager duchess lived up at The Hall
And her name was Ffoulkes-Ffarquarson-Simington-Small,
She spent oodles of time sitting on her veranda
With her cat she called Tiddles, or sometimes Miranda.

Miranda Ffoulkes-Ffarquarson-Simington-Small
Was a cat that was fat like a big fluffy ball,
And whenever the dowager slumbered and snored
Miranda miaowed and declared, 'I am bored!'

Now Tiddles Ffoulkes-Ffarquarson-Simington-Small
Decided one day she'd leap over the wall,
The dowager duchess implored her to stay,
But suddenly Tiddles was up and away.

Miranda Ffoulkes-Ffarquarson slid on the slides,
She swung on the swings and she joined the Girl Guides,
And soon she was slim and incredibly sleek
After doing aerobics three evenings a week.

Tiddles Simington-Small soon made friends with aplomb
And she even got chased by a gingerish tom,
She climbed up a tree, caught a mouse just for fun,
Which were things that before she would *never* have done!

Miranda Ffoulkes-Small let her fur down at night,
Getting out on the tiles, getting into a fight,
She did karaoke and sang out of tune
And she went to a party and burst her balloon.

But as all children know, things are not what they seem
And one day Miranda fell into a dream,
When Tiddles awoke she was back at The Hall
With kind Duchess Ffoulkes-Ffarquarson-Simington-Small.

Peter Davies

4th March

The Fledgling

A tiny head appears
Its beak agape
In the small round hole,
The entrance to the nest box.

A flurry of feathers,
Swift beat of wings,
As blue tit parents
Come to feed their young.

Soon these same parents
Perched upon a branch,
With loud repeated cheeps
Call to their young.

'Come out! Come out!'
They seem to cry,
'The whole wide world
Can be your home.'

A head appears and then retreats,
Then, hesitant at first,
The young one clambers up,
Balancing precariously.

His siblings jostling behind,
His balance lost,
He flaps and flaps his wings -
And flies - not very far!

But he is fledged,
The world is his,
As out his siblings tumble,
To join in his adventure.

Roma Davies

5th March

A Day In The Life . . .

Action men soar over the banister,
pencils slip down the side of the chair,
Lego scattered, jigsaws in a jumble,
the cat plays hide-and-seek under the table.
Half finished pages from colouring books,
biscuit crumbs finding all the nooks,
'Matchbox' and 'Hotwheels' everywhere,
dishevelled dolls and a teddy bear.
Odd socks, shoes hiding away,
they'll be found another day . . .
Cars zoom out across the landing,
Rollerblades creep forward . . . waiting . . .
Books on every available surface,
'Snap, crackle and pop' in every crevice.
Shouts and thumps, screams and wails,
things crash and my face pales . . .
Tears and tantrums, pushes and shoves,
cuddles and kisses, love yous and hugs.
'Mr Men' books, too many to count,
clothes on floor beginning to mount.
'Don't touch!', 'No!', 'Don't do that!'
out of the door races the cat.
Climbing up, falling down,
trips to casualty in town.
Crayons on the wall, 'It wasn't me . . .'
their art in evidence for all to see.
'Supernanny' on TV, Britney sings,
asking for quiet when the telephone rings.
They never had a volume switch,
so there's no change in fever pitch.
No handbook that carries the blame,
tomorrow, it'll just be the same . . .

5th March

Bedtime . . . elephants trumpeting up the stairs,
thumps and bumps, frowns and glares.
Downstairs, upstairs, down, then up again,
into bed, out of bed, 'One, two, three . . . ten!'
'Aren't they gone yet?' I'm holding my head!
Finally, tired little devils tucked up in bed.
Thumbs in mouths and teddies in arms,
sleeping like a lullaby written by Brahms.
Eyes shut, smiling like kings,
little angels, resting their wings.
No sooner than I drop into my chair
and stop tearing out my greying hair,
my eyes have dipped, my mind befuddled,
Sudoku? Forget it, I'm far too muddled.
My favourite programmes are on,
though I'm just too far gone,
I no longer care for their plight,
for in slumber I've lost the fight.
I'll sleep through their theme tunes,
even the ads' piercing booms,
and though hurricanes may bluster,
the only sound that I'll muster,
is the occasional snore,
'til a child opens the door . . .
'Mum . . .'

Lisa Shambrook

6th March

Just Wishing

Oh why was I born a little girl? I wish I was a boy,
I get dolls and girly things, I'd like a different toy.
Tomorrow is my birthday, I'll get such stupid things,
Why can't I have a skateboard or an aeroplane with wings?

I would like a nice big football to kick along the street
And a lovely water pistol to shoot everyone I meet.
Let me go and climb up trees, tear my best school shirt,
Please, why was I called Cynthia? I'd rather be Jack or Bert.

My cupboard's full with clothes for dolls, I don't want anymore,
Please buy me a nice fishing rod, a hammer and a saw.
I don't want that silly frock, it's pale blue jeans I'd like
And get rid of my old dolls' pram, I want a mountain bike.

Lipstick, powder and make-up, I really hate the smell,
I want a pair of football boots and a cricket bat as well.
One more thing I want from you, my really lovely mother,
I'd like someone to play with now, a lovely little brother.

Thomas Dickinson

7th March

I Thought

I thought I saw an elephant fly,
But it was only an aeroplane high in the sky.

I thought I saw a kangaroo hop,
But it was only Gran coming home from the shop.

I thought I saw a monkey skip,
But it was only a boy doing a backward flip.

I thought a saw a crocodile grin,
But it was only a dustman emptying the bin.

I thought I saw a polar bear jump,
But it was only a car riding over a bump.

I thought I saw a tiger prowl,
But it was only a postman with letters from town.

I thought I saw a pink pig roll,
But it was only my neighbour digging a hole.

All these things are a mystery to me,
I'll need new specs to help me see!

Angela Dolphin

8th March

The Panda, The Ostrich And The Kangaroo

One late morning, Missus Ostrich having laid two gorgeous eggs
invited Missus Panda home for brunch.
She offered her a spread of the tenderest bamboo shoots
available this side of the equator, dipped in virgin olive oil
Missus Panda, watching the two eggs from the corner of her eye
began to salivate abundantly
My, she thought, *what a fabulous omelette that would make scrambled, mmm*
I'm fed up of chewing the green stuff, I too need variety in my diet
Then Mr Kangaroo arrived, a little late
for he had some errands to run in the neighbourhood
Missus Ostrich had prepared for him a plate of radish mousse
and a salad of baby eucalyptus leaves
He too looked at her two eggs with envy, and visualised them fried
with onion rings, or, better still, with grated parmesan cheese
the way they're cooked in Macaroniland
Missus Panda read in his mind and exclaimed
'My God, someone has put a booby trap in your nest, quick, quick let's run for cover'
Alarmed, Missus Ostrich reacted instinctively burying her head in the sand
Missus Panda and Mr Kangaroo took advantage of the situation
and each left with one egg
'What a dumb bird,' said Missus Panda
'Indeed,' confirmed Mr Kangaroo, 'but she has the best eggs
I've ever tasted, and what's more, they're economical
it's a meal my whole little family will appreciate
'You're right,' said Miss Panda, 'it will last me a whole week.'

Albert Russo

9th March

Table Manners

Are you sitting comfortably,
Then children I'll begin
To tell the tale that adults wail,
'Their manners are in the bin!'

Don't scrape your chair dear.
Sit up straight,
Don't grab all the cakes dear,
But smile, and wait and wait.

Now put your napkin on your knee,
Don't slurp, don't burp,
Just look at me
When I'm talking to you.

I've told you once,
I've told you twice,
Talking with your mouthful
Just isn't nice.

But Mum, we don't understand
Why Dad does it and isn't banned
From elbows and slouching and dirty hands
This do as I say, not do as I do
Is confusing for us and the restaurant too!

Susan Carter

10th March

Noises Of The Night

A buzz of silence
A gush of wind
The creak of floorboards
A rustle of leaves
The patter of rain
The bark of a dog
The passing of a train
The croak of a frog
The call of an owl
The snap of a twig
The noises of creatures
All small and big
The footsteps of a stranger
The cry of a cat
The starting of an engine
The wings of a bat
A chilling sense of loneliness
And the threatening sense of silence
It's when you turn off the light
They are the noises of the night

Amy Clayton

11th March

There's A Fairy At The Bottom Of Our Garden

There's a fairy at the bottom of our garden . . .
she lives underneath the willow tree.
She has a pretty toadstool home - right next door to the gnome
and they play together, constantly.

As I crept down there - early one morning . . .
Gnome was fishing from the side of the pond
The fairy was swinging from the branches,
singing a most delightful song.

It was dawn so the birds joined in the chorus
and the rabbits hopped around on the lawn.
The fish swam right up to the surface
and the frogs watched over their spawn.

The grass was wet with dew and sparkling.
I saw lace-like cobwebs all around.
Then I tripped upon a twig which snapped and scared them . . .
Gnome quickly laid his fishing rod down.

The sound had disturbed them I could tell . . .
for an eerie silence fell over all.
Fairy flew back down to her toadstool
and Gnome stood very still and tall.

The rabbits darted into their burrows
and the birds stayed silent in the trees.
The fish dived down to the bottom of the pond . . .
and frog sat still upon the lily leaves.

Shhh, if you so much as whisper - you will frighten them.
You may only creep up and be . . .
as quiet as a mouse - as still as a stone -
then maybe one day they will let you see.

There's a fairy at the bottom of your garden . . .
hold Mummy's hand and she will take you to see.

Tomboy

Fairies

In the land where the fairies roam,
My mother said to me,
There are castles made of marshmallows,
That are very good to eat.
The floor is made of golden sand,
That twinkles like the stars,
The sky is very high
And a lovely shade of pink.
The clouds are white,
Like cotton balls,
That's where the fairies sleep.
They sleep when the sun goes down,
Like all good children do,
Then they wake up in the morn,
To the sound of *cock-a-doodle-do*.

So go to sleep my little child,
And in the morn you'll see,
The glowing sun,
The grass so green,
And flowers that smell sweet,
But do not forget,
My dear child,
The cock that crows so loud,
Do not be alarmed by him,
For he wakes up the fairies too.

Raghda Al-Jassar

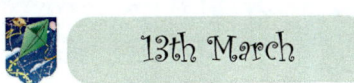

13th March

Untitled

Once, a little girl called Emi had a super wonderful dream,
It wasn't at all frightening, she didn't want to scream . . .
She dreamt she was a fairy, living in a nearby wood,
But she was very unhappy, though she always tried to be good.

There was a cruel old elf, selfish and feared by all,
Only a little bigger than the fairies but to them he was ten feet tall,
In the dream Emi was called Peri, she worked underground all day,
And by evening was so tired, she had nothing at all to say.

One day she was in the wood, because the old elf was in bed,
And suddenly a big blackbird, landed by her, smiled and said,
'If you want to be happy, Peri, climb on my back, do as I say,
I will take you to Tulip Land, where the skies are never grey.'

Peri clung on and the blackbird flew, she knew not where or why,
Only that to get away from the elf, she knew that she had to try . . .
In Tulip Land, she found each flower opened its petals by day,
And on the flattened surface, together all the fairies could play.

At night the petals closed up, providing each fairy with a bed,
But not 'til every single fairy, had been well and truly fed . . .
Peri settled down in Tulip Land, but Emi did not remember any more
Because at that moment she wakened,
    When her mum opened the bedroom door.

Robert H Quin

14th March

Little Green Giant

Little Arfur looked up at his mum and dad,
and his infant face became terribly sad.
For they towered above him, way up to the sky,
and he moaned, 'I'm only two feet high.'
He wrinkled his brow. He sighed. He frowned,
his head just two feet from the ground.

Delbert, his dad, was nine foot eight
and, at twenty-one stone, looked simply great;
Mimsy, his mum, just nine foot three
but some kilos heavier - no toothpick she.
With colossal shoulders and a smile cherubic,
she was built like a bus - distinctly cubic.

Little Arfur complained he was far too small
and vowed there and then to be ten foot tall.
'I'll eat loads of broccoli, heaps of beans,
cartloads of spinach and all my greens
and carbohydrates. I'll use the gym.
You see my dad? I'll be just like him.

You see my mum? I tell you what -
I, too, can resemble a juggernaut.'
So he wolfed down spinach and spuds in heaps,
shovelled in parsnips, cabbage, neeps,
lettuce, tomatoes, carrots, kale
and oodles of sprouts - he mustn't fail.

But, alas and alack, he just couldn't grow.
His increase in stature failed to show.
And - the weirdest thing you've ever seen -
his skin turned a bilious shade of green.
So he packed a suitcase and, leaving home,
applied for a job as a garden gnome.

Norman Bissett

15th March

Nursery Rhyme Mixture

Now old King Cole was a merry old soul
And the cat with his fiddle played rock and roll
For Tom, the piper's son, and the pig he stole

Little Boy Blue and Little Bo-Peep
Mary's lamb and baa, baa, black sheep
Collapsed in a heap and fell sound asleep

Georgy Porgy with a pocketful of rye
Saw twenty-four blackbirds in the sky
Instead of baked in a pudding or pie

Incy Wincy spider got lost one day
He met Miss Muffett eating her whey
She frightened him and he ran away

The clock went tick but did not tock
As three blind mice ran up the clock
And left the farmer's wife in shock

Rosemary Davies

16th March

My Edible Bedroom

I painted my walls with strawberry jam,
I tiled my floor with slices of ham.

I varnished my door with pink milkshake,
I made a doorknob with chocolate cake.

I crafted a bed from cheddar cheese,
I stuffed my pillow with mushy peas.

I painted my ceiling with chocolate spread,
I made some curtains from garlic bread.

I have a cover, it is toad in the hole,
I own a lamp made of Swiss roll.

I cuddle my ted who is made out of jelly,
I can't sleep here, it's way too smelly!

Tracy Green

17th March

My Shadow

I have a shadow that follows me
It goes everywhere I go
It has a heart of gold
Just like mine
I know it's there
When I'm lonely
And that cheers me up no end

I see my shadow on the wall
It goes everywhere I go
I can talk to it if I like
For it cannot answer me back
But I'm glad it's there
I'm not lonely no more
As I know it's looking after me

Ella Wright

18th March

Fat Neddy

There once was a Neddy, who lived in a field,
He sat in that field all day,
He ate and he ate all the grass he could get,
And farted his spare time away.

He swallowed and crunched,
He slurped and he munched,
Whatever poor soul crossed his path,
Until his owner, Annette, she called in the vet,
And poor Neddy would feel her wrath!

'This horse is too fat!' the vet she did cry,
'Exercise is the only solution,'
This proclamation adhered to all Neddy's fears,
The worst possible retribution.

And as for Annette, she tried and she tried,
To get our poor Neddy moving,
And because she was strong she could roll him along,
But Neddy really wasn't improving.

Neddy wheezed and he coughed at the torment,
But Annette was not giving up now,
He was put in a field, with little grass yield,
His only companion, a cow.

Now this cow, Daisy as we shall call her,
Though a sweetie, was really quite dumb,
So without conversation, to ease the situation,
To his fate, Neddy had to succumb.

But in the end all (but Neddy) were elated,
At the considerable weight reduction,
The process may have been slow, but effective although,
Neddy would have preferred liposuction.

 18th March

So with luck, this tale ended gladly,
And Annette can nowadays be seen,
Wandering to and fro, with Neddy close in tow,
Through grassy fields which remain lush and green.

And the moral of this story, it must be,
That pounds of weight are rather hard to shift,
So I'll use the motto, from Miss Piggy's muppet show,
And that's 'Don't eat more than you can lift'.

Naomi Thorne

19th March

A Snake In The Garden!

There's a snake in the garden
I saw it in the grass,
It was long and black
And it wouldn't let me pass.
Its tongue was pointed
And its eyes were all red,
It had stripes on its body
That went right to his head!
I'm sure I heard it hissing
As I took a closer look,
But you mustn't get too close
I read that in a book!
I think Dad ought to catch him
And take him right away,
I'm not sharing my garden
And I can't go out to play.
Dad's here now he'll be impressed
With the massive snake I've found,
But when he looks, he just laughs
It's a worm from under the ground!

P Hoddinott

20th March

Liverpudlian Pickings

'I'm making tea!' she said, our mam,
moving the tomatoes and the ham
to reach the worms in the yoghurt pot
at the back of our fridge.

'What we having?' my dad did ask
dropping down his newspaper mask
and shifting the spiders in the tub
from the arm of the chair.

'Ants,' she said, 'and locust wings.
Cockroach shells. Some other things.'
She brought them in piled on a plate.
They were good.
We ate
and ate.

Nick Kitching

A Crocodile!

Today I saw a crocodile;
it sat and stared at me!
I didn't run, I didn't shriek,
in case I was his tea!

No move I saw the snapper make,
his jaws remained tight shut.
Whilst sweat poured down my forehead,
I heard rumbles from his gut!

I've been in worse predicaments,
but only in my head.
Like wrestling with big brown bears,
and monsters from our shed!

The beast prepared to eat me up,
he snapped, he snarled, he blew!
But I just stood and tapped the glass,
'cause this croc was in the zoo.

Leon Adjarkoh (10)

22nd March

Don't Tell Mum

Dad gathered us all together one day
He said he had something important to say
'Whatever you see, pretend you are dumb
Whatever happens - just don't tell Mum!'

We nodded to let him know that we knew
Whatever it was he was going to do
That we could not see, that we would keep shtum
That we would not say a thing to Mum!

So it began, the disastrous day
Banging and crashing in every way
It's true we had butterflies in the tum
But remembered our promise not to tell Mum!

From the bathroom came an enormous flush
And water gushed down the stairs in a rush
We felt the tips of our fingers go numb
Yet resolved ourselves not to tell Mum!

But a noise from a car made us turn white
We searched for somewhere to hide in our fright
One thing was sure as we hid feeling glum
We would not have to say a word to our mum!

Pete Williams

23rd March

Mum's Best Boy

Oh how I love being me
My life is just perfect you see
My days are just bliss
And the reason for this
Is the love and affection from Mum

She takes care of all my needs
From brushing my hair to making my feeds
Not unusual you might say
This goes on every day
To show the love and affection from Mum

If I think I could be in trouble
I cry and Mum gives me a cuddle
To sit up on her knee
Is pure heaven for me
Getting love and affection from Mum

But there's a twist to this tale
For I'm a non-human male
I am a dog you see
But oh how I love being me!

Freda Clayton

24th March

My Mum Says

My mum says
Don't eat slugs,
Or any other bugs
That are slimy.

My mum says
It isn't very nice
To sit and nibble woodlice,
They are grimy.

My mum says
Don't lick up ants
They'll end up in your pants,
That's not a nice feeling.

My mum says
It's not all that wise
To go sucking up flies,
That are buzzing on the ceiling.

My mum says
Don't eat that fat worm,
But if I make it squirm
It stretches and gets thinner.

My mum says
It makes her feel unwell
To hear me crunching snail
And it puts her off her dinner.

I don't care 'cause I'm full up.

Marlene Parmenter

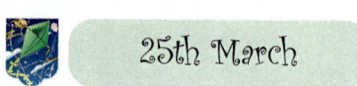

25th March

Do I Really Have To?

'Put your toys away,' says Mummy
'We are going out shopping today
Better get your wellingtons and mac
It's going to rain, so they say.'
I was happy playing on the floor
Watching my train go round the track
Do I have to put it all away now
It will take ages to put it all back.
Mummy said she would help me
If I did not make any more fuss
But we really had to leave now
As we would be missing the bus.
Mummy held my hand tightly
As we hurried along to the stop
She said I had been a good boy
And we could go and sit on the top.
Looking out of the misty windows
At the spots of water on the pane
Secretly hoping it wouldn't stop
I always loved walking in the rain.
When Mummy's shopping was over
She took me into the big toy store
'How about some rails and an engine?
I'm sure you could do with some more.'
So excited, I couldn't wait to get home
Dashing quickly through the front door
Mummy kept her promise to me
And the track was soon back on the floor.

Judith Watts

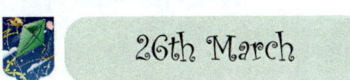

26th March

The Goblins

Goblins live in the forest so green
And although they are difficult to be seen
They're the grass on the ground, they're the leaves on a tree
Look very closely, a goblin you'll see.
Some goblins are bad, some goblins are good,
Some make you happy, some steal your food.
They tickle your nose, your ears, your knees
And they know itchy noses will make you sneeze.
And when you sneeze, a baby goblin is born
In the quiet and stillness of a forest dawn.

Susan Gordon

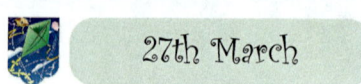

27th March

The Lonely Teddy Bear

The lonely teddy bear sat in the toy shop all alone,
He really wasn't happy, sat there with a frown
Little girls and boys had held him but put him back again,
Could be find someone to love him and take away his pain?

Next day a little girl came up to him,
He gave her such a cheeky grin,
'I'd love to take you home with me,' she said,
'Mummy will tell us lots of stories when we go to bed.'

Mummy replied, 'You can have the teddy for your birthday dear.'
So from now on the teddy had nothing to fear.
With hugs and kisses he felt so grand,
He was the happiest teddy bear in all the land.

Hazell Dennison

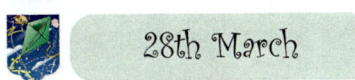

28th March

Little Green Men

There are little green men living in my garden.
I have seen them from my window just at dawn.
Gaily standing on their heads
In the furthest flower beds,
Or turning merry cartwheels on the lawn.

There are little green men living in my garden,
Always having fun and never sent to schools.
Chasing round the apple tree,
How I wish that one was me,
Not controlled by silly grown-ups, and their rules.

There are little green men living in my garden,
And their homes I cannot find, although I try,
So perhaps they go to bed
Snug inside our garden shed,
For that's the only place to keep them dry.

There are little green men living in my garden
And the only work I've ever seen them do
Is to spend the sunshine hours
Painting all our garden flowers.
My mum just says I'm lying, but it's true.

There are little green men living in my garden,
But my dad says such strange beings cannot be,
So I ask them in to play,
But they always run away.
Oh! Why can't grown-ups see them, just like me?

There are little green men living in my garden
Where they get involved in many pranks and tricks,
But when older folk come near
Strange to say, they disappear,
For adults and little green men do not mix.

Richard J Bradshaw

29th March

The Burger That Never Was

The sausage and the teacake met at the celery tree
And teacake said to sausage, 'Do you belong to me?'
Now sausage thought a little while and then replied, 'What's up?'
'We can't belong together, we have no red ketchup.'
So off they went together to find this very sauce.
Now this is where this poem ends, I'll tell you why because,
They came across a hungry boy whose name was Greedy Bill.
Before they knew what happened
Greedy Bill had had his fill.

E Wogden

30th March

Growing

The night my son was born I felt like a king
Such a beautiful innocent little thing
Dirty face and clothes and smelly nappy
But when he smiled we were so happy

I remember the day he took his first step
We were over the moon and almost wept
And as for the day he said his first word
A voice more like an angel has never been heard

Then his first day at the local school
In his little uniform he looked so cool
The years went by he grew big and strong
And with my help he learned right from wrong

Although he likes his music loud
He never ceases to make me proud
And if he sees a girl he thinks is nice
Then he comes to me for my advice

But all too soon he will leave our home
And set out to find a life of his own
Even then I still can't complain
A million memories will remain

Paul O'Boyle

31st March

Scamp

This is the story of a dog called Scamp,
who would not go walkies in the damp
when his mum said how do you do
he said be quiet, I'm having my chew.
Cor! I don't know which biscuits to choose
I think I'll lay on me beanbag and have a snooze,
but before I lay down with a plop
I'm going to scrounge a chocolate drop.

John Clarke

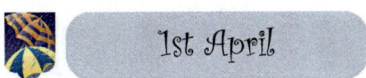 1st April

Rumble Rain

Who thumps on the pavement
Flows down the gutter
Runs down the drain?

Rumble Rain

Who drips down your window
Like tears from the clouds
Leaves tracks like a train?

Rumble Rain

Who runs down the streets
And goes through the pipes
Like blood rushing through a vein?

Rumble Rain

Who makes the field all muddy and wet
Puddles like saucers
Waters the grain?

Rumble Rain

Ryan Thomas (9)

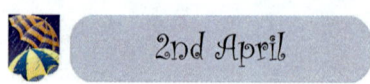

2nd April

Wally The Worm

Wally loved to poke his head through the soil
A new-found hobby of his,
Whoops that was a close one,
Nearly got me, did that starling!

What a good game, this is Wally thought,
Every morning do I show my head
Upon the soil's surface, risking life
Getting away with it every time.

But every day do I beat that starling,
For he is too slow to catch me,
Another score for this side,
Safe for another day.

But unknown to Wally,
Only the day before,
He had been observed with times,
Doing his daredevil tricks.

The fatal day did approach,
For Wally poked his head out,
Unaware of the blackbird,
That stood behind him waiting.

Wally was too slow this time,
The blackbird got him,
That was the last of Wally the Worm,
For he never thought of watching his back!

S J Davidson

3rd April

Ode To That Puddle

I need to find my booties,
I'm in a right kerfuddle,
I need to find my booties,
To jump into that puddle.

I need to find my booties,
I need to find them fast,
I need to find my booties,
While that puddle lasts.

I need to find my booties,
Before it is too late,
If I don't find my booties,
It will evaporate.

At last I've found my booties!
Alas it is in vain,
That puddle has dried up now,
I'll have to wait for rain.

At last I've found my booties!
I'm in a right kerfuddle,
Cos now I've found my booties,
I've gone and lost that puddle!

James Kitchener

4th April

Coltrane The Cat

Coltrane the cat sits in the rain
What's he doing?
Can he not feel the tip, tip tapping
The slish, slish slashing
Of jagged raindrops on his back?
Poor tabby. Stupid tabby.
Body hunched up like a ball
With a head.
Triangular ears, attached
Prick, pricky, pricked up
They twitch.
Psst, psst. Pussycat! Pussycat!
Can he not hear?
Come inside the warm.
Psst! Psst!
This is more than I can bear.

At last!

He turns his head
Thump. He jumps,
Paws hit the deck
Trit-trot, trit-trot, trit-trot
A quick look behind him
Perhaps one last check.

In through the door
Cat footprints on the kitchen floor
Four by four, by four,
Spiky fur, spiky, standing on end
A David Beckham Mohican on the top of his head
Shaky, shaky, shaking his fur
Wall and floor sprayed, wet with rainwater.
Before he heads my way
To coil his wet body around my legs
I dish out the cat food.

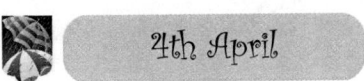 4th April

No need for him to be shooed
Coltrane, my tabby
Fully fed, sitting pretty on my lap
Grooms his body
Until, he no longer looks shabby.

Carmen Emmanuelle

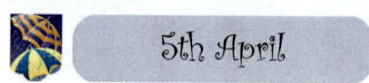 5th April

Worm Squirm

A worm lives in my garden,
his name is Squirmy Steve,
he digs the soil for me
and tidies up the leaves.

A tunnel building expert,
he's the perfect shape to slide
back inside his earthy hole
when he decides to hide.

His face is not the cutest,
he only has a mouth,
in fact it's really hard to tell
his north end from his south.

That's why he puts a hat on -
then everybody knows
the end that's best to talk to
is wearing trendy clothes.

So if you ever notice
a small worm in a hat
stop and talk to Squirmy -
he's hoping for a chat.

Jan Harris

 6th April

Falling Rain

I like the sound of falling rain
Especially when it hits my windowpane
Outside there's puddles on the ground
After all the rain has fallen down

When the rain has gone the sun comes out
The little children all run about
They play hide-and-seek and peekaboo
Hold hands and sing ring-a-roses too.

Hazel Davies

 7th April

Early Bird/Hungry Worm

Two earthworms were talking
One to the other said,
'Let's move from here, now!
To next-door's flower bed.'

'Why?' asked the contented worm.
'I'm starving,' his friend said,
'Instead of looking for food here
Let's enjoy the fertilised bed.'

'Try and pull yourself together,
You really are not thin,
You are just stretched out
So head to tail pull in.'

'Will that stop my hunger,
This longing me to fill?'
'Maybe will, perhaps will not
But this blackbird coming will.'

T W Denis Constance

8th April

Toad

Poor old toad lived all alone
In the dark beneath the shed.
Then someone came, removed his home,
And made a compost heap instead.

He found some rotting wood and crawled
Beneath its friendly cover,
When that home went he was appalled
And tried to find another.

Toad crawled away behind the weeds
But they were soon ripped out.
No one cared for poor toad's needs -
It was a poor lookout.

Toad crawled away to pastures new;
He had no goods to pack.
It was the only thing to do,
But maybe he'll be back.

Chris Gutteridge

The Bluebird

Lonely bluebird in the clear blue sky,
Travelling with the warm sunny breeze
As you fly so high,
Wandering past those misty white clouds,
Searching for the treasure at the rainbow's end.

I wonder if you're looking down on the land,
Choosing where to build a dream one day,
Finding your paradise where you are home to stay,
Tending to your hatchlings where they are safe to play.

Or are you an angel,
Making dreams come true,
Spreading your magic across the land below,
Leaving a trail of daisies that glow,
In the magical gardens of the world I know?

Camille Metcalfe

10th April

A Window Friend

A wee girl sat watching the rain,
As its droplets trellised the windowpane,
Gleefully running, they chased each other,
Avoiding splashes so as not to smother.
But they joined as a brooklet slipping down,
Like sparkling dew on a fabulous gown.
Some of the rainfall made a map,
Then it joined hands to fill the gap.
When they wandered and whirled as eddies flow,
Or briefly as winds where rushes grow.
They massed together, deciding to make,
That pit-a-pat rain, so wide awake.
It told a story of rainbow's end,
And the girl at the window who waved to her friend.

Tom Cabin

11th April

In The Land Of Never-Never . . .

In the wonderful land of Never-Never . . .
  where children's laughter is the glowing sun;
    there is a beautiful place - for little children,
      whose needs are met, by lots and lots of fun.

    Scrumptious toffee trees; grow in wild abundance;
  with ice cream bushes, growing around,
  soda fountains, create colourful rainbows . . .
whilst milkshake rivers, are so easily found.

In the land of Never-Never . . .
  there no child ever goes to bed;
    for in this place - of sheer contentment,
      there could never be a weary head.

    There is no child experiences, grief nor sadness;
  there is no one endures, grief or pain -
  because in this land, where dreams lay rested . . .
milk and honey; are the falling rain . . .

I've seen houses, built from milk chocolate;
  with pavements, laid with spearmint bars . . .
    A horse quite greedily, ate up a lamp post;
      now all is lit up, by the evening stars . . .

    In the wonderful land of Never-Never . . .
  where special children, all go to play -
  there is never, the night or a sign of darkness,
for happiness is simply; one long day . . .

I chance visited, this place of sunshine . . .
  and I was lucky, all the wonders to share . . .
    in the beautiful land of Never-Never . . .
      when as a boy; my dreams strayed there . . .

Thomas Ian Graham

 12th April

Passion Of A Boy

Before I go to sleep
I'll count sweets instead of sheep
Mum says; they are bad for my teeth
Without them my life would not be complete

I like fruity chews and jelly tots
Smarties and desserts in pots
My favourite are transparent snakes
Must not forget yummy Cadbury's Flakes

An ice cream cone with sauce on top
Washed down by some fizzy pop
A packet of crisps and popcorn too
I had so much fun at the zoo

Sometimes I'll dream of Turkish Delight
Or climbing candy mountains at night
Skiing down an ice cream slope
Being rescued by a liquorice rope

For now I'll have rainbow sherbet for my sky
And chocolate aeroplanes flying by
I'll sculpt a big yellow moon from ice
Use candyfloss clouds, marshmallow mice

My picture will let all see
How magic my passion can be

Eileen Kyriacou

13th April

Chocolate Mountain

I wish I had a chocolate mountain,
with peardrops raining on its peak,
and slow-flowing caramel rivers,
and all the candy one could seek.

Knights jousting with candy canes,
by the wishing well on Lollipop Lane,
and dance on truffles by the lake,
filled with icing sugar from Spain.

Dragons breathing hot soft fudge,
before dancing to mid-west blues,
and winning a sugar paper award,
and a prize of penny chews.

Marc E Wright

14th April

Gertrude (Who Wouldn't Stop Eating And Eventually Exploded)

Gertrude was a girl who was not very tall,
Everyone remarked, 'She's so tiny and small!'
Of course no one meant to be mean and unkind,
But it sounded so unfair in Gertrude's mind.
All of her classmates were really quite tall,
And in no game included her at all -
So Gertrude arrived home that day, deep in thought,
And her mother's advice she earnestly sought.
'Mother, please tell me why I'm so small.'
But her mother simply dismissed it all
By saying, 'Eat up your tea and you'll grow up, you'll see.'
So this was the start of it - oh dear me!

Gertrude made an effort to eat her food,
She ate and she ate, whatever her mood,
And gobbled and gorged and wouldn't stop,
Until everyone said that one day she'd pop.
She chewed and she munched from noon until night,
Even in her sleep, she would crunch and bite.
She ate up her peas and lots of green beans,
Her entrées, her afters and in-betweens.

Salmon mousse or baked stuffed trout,
Chestnut stuffing and Brussel sprouts,
Vegetable lasagne and chicken soup,
And for pudding, orange soufflé with chocolate gloop.
Whatever she saw, she devoured on sight,
And grew simply ginormous overnight.

As her teeth sank into that last meringue,
There was a *fizz* and a *spark* and an almighty *bang!*
With a crackle and rainbow shower so bright,
The chandelier fell and out went the light.
Gertrude gave a yell, and a deafening shout,
But alas she had exploded right out of sight!

Rachel Gowdy

 15th April

The Caramel Camel

With sugar-coated teeth
And breath so sweet
The caramel camel
Is rarely seen.
Such tasty lumps
Those caramel humps
On desert plains
This camel runs.
On dunes of jelly
His caramel belly
And chocolate hooves
That set like mousse.
A fudge-like mammal
Half pudding, half animal
A delicious treat
The caramel camel.

Craig Shuttleworth

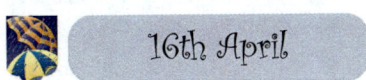 16th April

Tooth Fairy

There is a story I must tell
about a tooth fairy named Chelsea Bell
with long blonde hair and eyes so blue
when you lose a tooth she will come to you
late at night when it is dark and still
she flies through the window and waits until
all the children are fast asleep
under the pillow she does a peep
she pops the tooth into her sack
and leaves a coin putting the pillows back
quiet and gentle, you don't hear a thing
as Chelsea flies and flaps her wings
she flies off into a magical land
where she turns your teeth into pearly white sand
so remember the next time you lose a tooth, a visit you will get
I know who from, can you guess?
Yes, the tooth fairy, Chelsea Bell
and this story you too can tell

Allison Bell

17th April

Creation

In long ago darkness space gave birth
To a grim grey planet it named the Earth.

A throbbing sun lit the inky blue
Which prickled with stars when the moon shone through.

With a rushing gush and a roaring rave
Came the pluming, spuming, fuming wave.

Stretching, reaching from strong young roots
Poked the fresh green saplings' shining shoots.

Then teeming, reaming, the sea was rich
With flickering fish in a shimmering twitch.

With feathers and fur wild creatures grew
And they leapt or crept or ran or flew.

And humans walked on the brand new soil.

And the Earth is ours to love or spoil.

Jane Bower

 18th April

Vanity

In the garden of a house, where the owner hated cats,
there was a swimming pool.
Every evening when people indoors dined, laughed and drank wine
a tiny mouse went to the poolside to see its own reflection;
it looked so tall, it thought bigger than the neighbour's tomcat
and it had dreams of conquering the world.
Disaster struck, when leaning forward to get closer to its own image
it slipped and fell into the water,
the poolside so slippery it couldn't get up.
Vast this dead ocean, where no fishes swam
or seaweed danced with the current.
Unjust struggle with only one possible outcome,
but miracles do happen,
a gust of wind, a wave threw it exhausted back on shore;
alas, the neighbour's cat was there and it was huge.

Jan Oskar Hansen

 19th April

Snow White

In a long time ago before you and I
Lived a princess whose beauty was praised to the sky
The queen was angry and her magic mirror told
Snow White was more beautiful than the rarest gold

The queen planned to kill her, so with a woodcutter she sent
Snow White to the forest, this foul deed, his intent
But her gentleness melted his cold, cold heart
That he set her free into the forest so dark

She then found a cottage and went fast asleep
Not knowing the seven dwarfs owned this retreat
On their return they were overcome
By this shy, lovely girl they would come to love

They all lived together happy and content
Till the evil queen vowed Snow White's life was spent
The queen dressed as a gypsy and sold apples so red
Snow White took just one bite and fell as though dead

As she lay and people mourned her a prince then rode by
He kissed the beautiful princess then as he cried
Her eyes began to open and love filled their hearts
From that very moment, they knew they'd never part

Gillian Mullett

 20th April

Dragon's Breath

If you wish to see a dragon
your heart must first believe
and your sword must be abandoned
and left within its sheath.
Words of truth be spoken
an allegiance sworn
so when, your eyes are fully open
the dragon will suspend,
its hide-and-seek traditions
that stand on view, untamed,
and you'll see your first dragon
breathe a mighty sheet of flames,
across the cold horizon
and our green and pleasant land,
so what others, will have just imagined
you'll have witnessed at first hand.

Alan Glendinning

 21st April

Dinner Guests

A tiger with claws of bright steel,
Invited a deer to a meal,
But the wise deer wrote back,
'Yes I may for a snack,
But I seldom consort with a male.'

The next guest he asked - a giraffe
Turned her slow long neck, with a laugh,
And said in reply,
'On leaves that are high,
I usually dine - not on beef!'

A monkey hung up by her tail,
The tiger then sought to regale,
With, 'I've succulent meat
In my cave, come and eat.'
But she said, 'Ha! I'm no numskull.'

'Damn me,' said the tiger, 'what a nerve
These animals have. I observe
My tactics are faulted,
If they are not altered
I fear that I surely must starve!'

The moral of this lyric verse,
Is simple as sunlight, of course,
If you're asked out to dine
With a tiger - decline!
Or you'll certainly come off worse!

Alan C Brown

From An Acorn . . .

Dear child
You have a tale to tell
Your smile and charm
You cast a spell

Your face
It shines
A glow
It beams
A simple tale
Of life
And dreams

Grow up strong
And you will be
As sturdy as
An old oak tree

So try your hardest
Do your best
Let love and luck
Do the rest

Mark Guy

Untitled

Sitting cross-legged on the warm, warm lawn
With a tickle on my leg
And a lazy little yawn,
I am looking at a bee
Who is looking back at me and
I wonder what it must be like.

Is it good to be a bee in the warm, warm sun?
Is it easy finding flowers,
Is busy buzzing really fun?
Is it fun to fly around
Making busy buzzing sounds, oh
I wonder what it must be like.

Lying flat out on the daisy lazy lawn
With a tickle in my nose
And a lazy little yawn,
I look up at a bird
Who is looking down at me and
I wonder what it must be like.

Is it good to be a bird in the windy, windy sky?
Is it fun looking down
When you're up, up high?
It must be good to swoop,
Flying round and round in loops, oh
I wonder what it must be like.

Sitting on the ground in the cool, cool breeze
With a rumble in my belly
And a loud, loud sneeze,
I think about the children
With no homes or hopes or fun
And I wonder what it must be like.

Fiona Spotswood

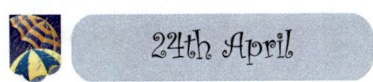

Concerning Dreams

I wonder can you tell me,
Are your dreams long or small?
Do you dream every night?
Or don't you dream at all?

Also please can you tell me,
Are your dreams in black and white?
Like a television set,
Are they in colour yet?

Another question please answer,
Do they ever come true?
Are they just fantasies?
And are they ever blue?

Some dream of unpleasant things,
With no hope and despair,
Some dream lovely dreams,
Some horrible nightmares.

We dream just before we wake,
That's what all the experts say,
Dreams seem to last all night,
Sometimes during the day.

So when next you dream, tell me,
So that I can then respond.
In answer to those questions,
That I have pondered upon.

Terry Daley

 25th April

Flight Of The Chickens

Entering the petrol station
Tipsy chickens on vacation
Tiny bantams on a dare
Sip unleaded with great care
Finding themselves not quite dead
Guzzle diesel, mixed with bread
Soon the pumps are fully drained
Bantam bellies slightly strained
Sloshing off into the night
A foolish fowl strikes a light
Whoosh! With somewhat startled stare
Chickens zooming through the air
A petrol-powered poultry rain
Till all had struck the earth again
Some of them were slightly fatter
Still it didn't seem to matter
Scraping themselves from off the ground
(With a handy spatula they'd found)
And swigging down another beer
They vowed to come again next year

Sandra Bates

 26th April

Given Away

Where were you on parents' night?
Duty day again
And when the school bazaar was held
Why were you away?
Report due in I expect and
I'm a social worker's kid

When I read my play to you
Why were you asleep?
And when the field trip returned home
Why was I the last?
Conference on, ran over and
I'm just a social worker's kid

The tea is late
The house a mess
But we can wait
And we can guess
When you'll be back

Where were you on Saturday?
Another report?
And when I went to bed that night,
You were writing still
I read myself to sleep and said
I'm a social worker's kid

When I'm asked what will I do?
I will tell them all
Not a social worker, never that -
To make my children feel
Other kids counted more and my time
Could be given away.

Jessica Bartlett

27th April

Mr Zippy

Mr Zippy is in town,
Mr Zippy, the famous clown,
His face is painted yellow and red,
A purple parrot sits on his head.

Mr Zippy's eyes are green,
He's the tallest clown you've ever seen,
His legs are so long! His feet so big!
His boots are brown boxes, his hair a white wig.

Mr Zippy wiggles his ears,
Walks on his hands, cries buckets of tears,
He takes giant footsteps, falls into a hole,
Slithers and slides down a long greasy pole.

Mr Zippy laughs a lot,
On the end of his nose is a bright blue spot,
He presses a button on his chest,
And a fountain of water spurts out of his vest.

The children laugh, the children scream,
He's the funniest clown they've ever seen.
Today the circus tent came down,
Mr Zippy is leaving town.

Mr Zippy has gone away,
He said he'd come back another day.

Emelie Buckner

28th April

Can You Keep A Secret?

Can you keep a secret?
I'm pretty sure you can!
It's all about the garden
And a little Goblin Man.
He works among the flowers
But he's very hard to see
Because he is so tiny
Not big, like you and me.

His job is never-ending
And he's busy all year through,
With mixing pots and brushes,
There's such a lot to do!
He has some willing helpers,
Three pixies and two elves,
Who hold the little bluebell pots
And mix the paint themselves.

Now when you see the raindrops
And the sun peeps through as well,
Here's the magic secret
You must promise not to tell!
The Goblin sends the pixies
And the elves away on high
To collect the brilliant colours
From the rainbow in the sky.

They paint each velvet petal
In orange, red or blue,
With indigo and violet
And heaps of yellow too;
And every leaf in shades of green
Completes the Master's plan,
Bringing beauty to your garden
From the little Goblin Man.

Pat Watson

29th April

Well Rounded Citizens

Prayed my children's lives would be different to mine,
Spent hours playing with them, having quality time.
Took them on journeys to places of interest,
On holidays went to the seaside, liked this best.

Tried to impress the need of good education,
Jobs offered to one with great qualification.
But of course, they all rebelled and went their own way,
At last, years later, believed what I used to say.

Without grades needed, they find it hard to survive,
Though they became well rounded citizens aged five.

S Mullinger

The Blackbird Sings The Blues

(Alice's poem)

O Blackbird what joy you bring,
Your song would wake the dead,
What are those words you 'blithely' sing.
That dragged me from my bed.
The cats were noisy all night through,
The owl tu-whit tu-whooed
And now each morning starts like this,
What can a poor mouse do?
The cats miaul; the owls tu-whits,
The blackbird sings the blues,
The cows are mooing for their lunch,
A dog's now barking too.
The doves are fluttering on the roof,
The thunder rumbles loud -
I wish my ears were very small
And tucked away inside . . .

Robert Carson

1st May

Lost And Found

A poor lonely garden gnome
Out in all weathers, he had no home
Spending each day just ambling around
At night fell asleep on the cold muddy ground
Soon his bright clothes were worn away
No other gnomes asked him to play
Dirty and scruffy he continued to roam
He longed for a place he could call home
A boy found him lying face down in the mud
Took him back home and gave him a scrub
Now looking pale the boy knew what to do
He painted the gnome with a coat so blue
The gnome now looked almost like new
The boy placed him in the garden for all to view
Alongside another well painted gnome
Now placed together they are never alone.

L A G Butler

 2nd May

Dizal

Dizal the dog was as daft as a brush
When he waggled and chased his tail in a rush
He'd jump up and down as he barked while he raced
With a big sloppy grin on his big woolly face
All around and around in a whirl he would go
Always too fast and never too slow
In circles and spirals of dust he would run
'Cause chasing his tail was such dizally fun!

Louise Hercules

3rd May

Billy's Little Engine

The little engine was very slow
Coughing and spluttering all the way
Billy started crying
What is matter with you today?
It was his most precious toy
The little engine and its trucks
Chugging through the village
Past the pond with ducks
Now it wasn't quite itself today
No power to take it uphill
Billy sat there crying
Very sad until
Mother came and saw their plight
Not liking to see them sad
She quickly put things right
The little engine's wheels were dirty
Collecting fluff from off the floor
She soon cleaned them off again
And quietly closed the door

Daphne Fryer

4th May

Caveman Chaos

Tap, tap, chip, chip, caveman's thrill
As it rolled, he created the wheel.
To his delight, there was no pause,
He didn't realise the chaos it would cause.

Bumper to bumper, but not getting far,
Lorries, vans and the humble car.
One by one, they wait their turn,
Nobody cares about the fuel they burn.

Inch by inch, they take their patch,
Another traffic jam, the latest batch.
One way, no way, grockles' bounty,
Buy a map, study the county.

Tow truck, slow truck, someone broke down,
To the garage, a driver's frown.
Blue lights, headlights, sirens a-blare,
The traffic slows and people stare.

Red light, green light, stop and start,
The amber's there to serve what part?
We drive like the tortoise, but act like the hare,
We're all on the roads, we begrudge to share.

Anthony Hayward

5th May

Little Button Daisy

Little Button Daisy was a very small baby
Who slept in a glove in a drawer
She was pretty and sweet and very petite
Her parents could not ask for more
She was just an hour old, or so it's been told
A flower fell down from the sky
Her hand caught its stem and that is just when
A magical breeze wafted by
But not only that a strange looking cat
Wearing pearl button collar and shoes
Slinked in on the breeze just as bold as you please
With a scroll of incredible news
His name was Willard and his job was to guard
Button Daisy throughout every hour
As she'd been appointed with magic anointed
To become the new 'Princess of Power'
Her role was to bake 'The Happiness Cake'
To share with the poor and the needy
With Willard in tow she'd set off and go
In a wheelbarrow bus called 'The Feedy'
With a wave of her daisy she'd wake up the lazy
And sprinkle their world with perfume
Casting magical spells with a bouquet of smells
And ridding the shadows of gloom
She would travel the seas for her magic to please
And spread calm in the countries of war
Her cute little smile smiling every mile
To promote what a smiley smile's for
And Willard would be by her side constantly
With his pearl button collar and shoes
And together they'd journey the straight and the turny
Creating a world of good news

David Whitney

6th May

Paul Thomas

Paul Thomas is a little lad who likes to play with cars,
And when he goes to bed at night he plays amongst the stars.
His bedroom is a fortress and no one can get in,
Unless they know the password and then he lets them in.
Inside is a land just made for children where giant pigs do fly,
Clouds are made of candyfloss and crepe paper makes the sky.
The birds all sing in chorus, they sing the nicest songs,
There are no strangers here and everyone belongs.
Jelly trees do bounce about and popcorn is the craze,
Lemonade pools are all about and ice pops make the maze.
The cats are made of treacle, dogs are made of honey,
Everybody loves them because they are so funny.
Houses of marshmallow stand next to the station bold,
The trains are made of marzipan, at least that's what I'm told.
Mountains made of chocolate rise until they reach the sky,
Rocks on them won't hurt you, they are made of apple pie.
It's a land just made for children, it's a world of make-believe,
Use your imagination and see what you can see.
Paul Thomas, Paul Thomas you're a friend indeed.
Let me come and join you in your world of make-believe.

Don Goodwin

7th May

My Folly Cryptic Adventures

My favourite frolly locus
Nature cryptic adventures tell
Where I adore to visit
In the heart of the dell

Humble creatures I befriend
Luminous beady eyes share
Squirrels, rabbits and mice
Their affable presence share

Judicious tawny owl
Tu-whit, tu-whoos me to stay
Impudent elves and pixies
Dance around me and play

Towering giant trees bow
Merging rippling rivers flow
Abundance of wild flowers
Bearing pretty heads grow

Spiking hedgehogs rustle by
Ladybirds and insects creep
Spellbound toads and frogs
Elusive fairies hide and peep

Patricia Carter

8th May

Myrtle The Turtle

There once was a turtle
And her name was Myrtle
Who laid forty eggs in the sand.
Then, pleased as could be
She went off to tea
Saying, 'I think large families are grand.'
She had a nice tea
But oh! Dearie me!
She forgot where her eggs had been laid
And she got so upset,
'Just how could I forget
Where I left all my babies?' she said
'For I left them at noon
If I don't find them soon
I fear they'll wash out with the tide,'
And she hunted around
But they couldn't be found
So the poor turtle sat down and cried.
Then close by at hand
From out of the sand
Came forty small turtles, in line
Then pleased as can be
She cried, 'Oh! Dearie me,
Aren't my lovely babies divine.'

Gordon Andrews

9th May

The Spider

'Come into my parlour,'
Said the spider to the fly
'You look like you could use some tea
And I have some scrumptious pie.'

'May I sit by the window?'
The fly said to the spider
'Would you mind opening
The curtains, just a little wider

I do so like the sunlight,'
The fly said with a smile
But the spider's mind was elsewhere
For a little while

'I'm sorry,' said the spider
'The curtains did you say?
Could we not adjust them
I prefer them left this way?'

The fly felt just a little peeved
At his host's reply
And asked, 'Do you prefer the darkness
Would it be rude to ask you why?'

'Well,' replied the spider
'It's only natural for me
I suppose it's in my make-up
The way I'm meant to be'

The fly, not yet convinced
Said, 'It must be difficult to see
You know, when you're eating
Or having guests for tea'

'Don't be silly,' said the spider
'It's all the same to me
Whether I'm having dinner
Or a fly for tea!'

Georgina Paraskeva

9th May

10th May

Fairyland

Have you seen the little elves
Down in yonder glen?
Watch them, see them tripping quickly
In and out the fen.

Have you seen the sprightly fairies
'Mongst the dewdrops still,
Sipping nectar from the roses
Growing on the hill?

Have you watched the moonlight pixies
Sitting near a rill?
Down amongst the purple heather
When the night is still?

If you want to watch them dancing
When the dawn is near
Come and watch, but do not scare them
Lest they flee through fear.

Valma June Streatfield

11th May

Where Have All The Spiders Gone?

Where have all the spiders gone?
I'm sure I saw one here,
I'm sure they were here yesterday,
They can't just disappear.

I checked in every room you know,
I checked through every door,
I like to keep my eye on them,
In case they abseil to the floor.

I've seen them all and named them all,
The ceilings were pretty scary,
Still, the spiders were my pets you know,
Despite them being hairy.

I know that spiders move around,
I know each one is a mover,
But; guess what, just guess?
Mum has sucked them up the Hoover!

Wanderer watched me from his web,
Spinderly lived in the *living* room
Bungee Jumper practised by the loft,
Now they all rest in a Hoover-bag tomb.

RIP.

Alex Brown (aged 8) & Mummy (aged a lot more)

12th May

The Circus

My dad says a circus has come to town,
    with lions and tigers and even a clown.
If we've been good children, then maybe we'll go,
    I'm sure that my mum will enjoy the show.

I've been there before and remember such things,
    some ladies were flying without any wings.
A lady rides bare-back upon a white horse,
    there's elephants and monkeys and jugglers of course.

When the circus is over we'll go to the fair,
    Dad often wins coconuts when we go there.
I'll try catching ducks at that nice lady's stall,
    I might win a goldfish and buy him a bowl.

One thing I must buy, I just can't resist,
    some pink fluffy candyfloss would round a stick.
It's time to go home now we've had a great day,
    I'll tell all my friends when I go out to play.

I've bought goldfish food so I hope he won't die
    because if he did I know I would cry.
When I go to bed, I'm not going to cry
    I'll dream of that lady and wish I could fly.

J Windle

13th May

Fairies' Day Of Work

After a long hard day
Of painting the Lord's rainbow
The fairies fall asleep
After a little nap the fairies bathe and wash all the paint off

The next job is to have tea ready for the Lord
They fly across the big long table and put a nice clean cloth on it
And lots of fruit bowls all around, then freshly cut flowers spread all over.

Then the fairies change into all their finery
To accompany the Lord at his table.

After eating it's time to play
They fly around the Lord sitting on his lovely long hair
Some even bounce off his tummy
Some even take off his shoes
And pull the thread off his socks

The fairies think all this is fun
The good Lord just laughs with them

He knows quite soon he will have to take them all to bed
He knows that these fairies have had a busy day.

Sleep tight for I will be here all night.

Debbie Storey

14th May

Mr Greenjacket

My name is Mr Greenjacket, I live in an old well,
I make shoes for the fairies down by the dell.
I've got wriggly fingers, and wriggly toes,
And if you want a pair of shoes I can make you some of those.

I can make them to fit, I can make them just like that,
I can make you a fine pair of shoes with a rat-a-tat-tat-tat-tat.

Then one morning the king of the fairies, he said to me -
'Hello Mr Greenjacket, can you make for me,
A saddle for my horse, a bridle and some reins,
And can you make them in white leather, to match my horse's mane?'

I can make them to fit, I can make them just like that,
I can make you a fine saddle with a rat-a-tat-tat-tat-tat.

Then one morning the queen of the fairies, she said to me,
'Hello Mr Greenjacket, can you make for me,
A brand new pair of shoes for the fairy ball?
For I have no nice shoes, no, no, none at all.'

I can make them to fit, I can make them just like that,
I can make you a fine pair of shoes, with a rat-at-tat-tat-tat-tat.

Then this morning I got my invite to the fairy ball,
But I have no nice jacket, no, no, none at all.
Dewdrops for the buttons lined with dandelion fluff,
Sewn with the finest silk, and tulips for the cuffs.

I can make it to fit, I can make it just like that,
I can make myself a fine jacket, with a rat-a-tat-tat-tat-tat.

My name is Mr Greenjacket, I live in an old well,
I make shoes for the fairies down by the dell.
I've got wriggly fingers, and wriggly toes
And if you want a pair of shoes I can make you some of those.

I can make them to fit, I can make them just like that,
I can make just about anything, with a rat-a-tat-tat-tat-tat.

Emma Lockyer

15th May

Hey Look, I'm An Earwig!

To succeed as an earwig
takes faith more than pluck.
You've got to believe
that it isn't just luck
when shoes do not crush you
to nasty brown jam.
You've got to think, hey -
see how handsome I am!
Apart from the Buddhists
(who never kill ants)
most folks step on crawlies
when they have the chance.
So, if you travel further
from here, say, to there;
and nobody steps
on your long derrière,
you're entitled to think
it's respect you've been shown,
and go on your way;
faith, as yet, still unblown.

Roy Tuvey

 16th May

Bee Team

Hello Mr Furry Bee,
Please will you answer me -
I really like your stripy strip
As round amongst the flowers you sip,
It's not a colour I have seen
So which please is your favourite team?

Hive United is my team,
Of all the league they are the cream,
But we don't have much time to play
Gathering nectar all the day . . .
That's why when my stripes you see,
Cheer for honey with your tea!

Di Bagshawe

17th May

Getting Bigger

I've grown in the night, I must have!
I'll measure against the wall.
Now I can reach the light switch.
Last try, I couldn't at all.

That shelf that was too high, the last time,
I find I can reach now with ease.
I'll reach now myself, not ask Mummy.
She'll get a surprise when she sees.

My sister still hasn't grown yet.
She can't reach that high shelf.
She can't even reach the light switch,
So I'll do it for her, myself.

I expect very soon I shall grow some more.
I'll be able to reach really high,
Then things I couldn't, like yesterday,
I reach like today, at first try.

Pauline Boncey

18th May

Chop! Chop!

Old George was a butcher
He had a village store
He'd built a reputation
Over thirty years or more
His small shop held the finest
In beef and pork and lamb
His poultry was all local
As were his joints of ham
George ran his little empire
With his young assistant, Drew
They got on like a house on fire
Then he found pastures new
But new assistant, Jack
Had raised in George, some doubts
Money was missing from the till
George mused on its whereabouts
Then one day George had him
Jack stood frozen still
He had been caught red-handed
With his hands deep in the till
It quickly dawned on George
His senses did awaken
He'd be a silly sausage
If he saved Jack's bacon
He had to keep up standards
Within his butcher's shop
His cleaver hacked a piece of pork
And he gave young Jack the chop.

Paul Spender

 19th May

Ogg!

'Neath gorsey hedgerows lives a hog
A hedgehog by the name of Ogg.
Dear Ogg has spines upon his back
To ward off any cruel attack
And when he harkens danger's call
Fast rolls up in a prickly ball.

In wintertime when cruel winds blow
And humans brave rain, hail and snow,
Ogg sleeps and dreams the time away
'Neath rotting leaves till springtime gay
Awakens him with sweet bluebells
To roam again the fairy dells.

Ogg often goes on nightly jaunts
To all his favourite leafy haunts
Roots long for grubs to heart's content
But times he goes where he's not meant.
Crossing a busy motorway
Oft ends a hedgehog's happy day.

Violet M Corlett

20th May

Lonely Tree

At the bottom of my garden,
There stands a lonely tree,
In the darkness of the night,
I hear him call to me,
'Come outside and let us play,
In the light from the moon,
But hurry now, don't delay,
The sun is coming soon.'
I scurry to the garden,
Wanting now to play,
When I reach his big dark trunk,
I only here him say,
'I have a riddle, answer quick,
And we can play by night.
It is easy; it's no trick,
But you must get it right.'
I ponder this and nod my head,
Clear my brain of thought,
I glance around at my house,
I just cannot get caught.
'You can hear me, you can feel me,
I push the clouds around the sky,
But I'm so cunning, you can't see me,
What on this earth am I?'
I cross my fingers and close my eyes,
As a breeze stirs the night,
I know the answer, I know I have it,
'It's the wind, am I right?'
'Oh, you are a clever one,
I really have to say.
Come along; let's have some fun,
It will soon be day.'

M Rae

21st May

Itsy Bitsy

Itsy Bitsy Missy Moo
went down the lane one day,
to visit Aunt Matilda
who sometimes let her play

in the meadow full of daisies
where old Jonah sometimes stood
watching Itsy Bitsy
as he chewed upon his cud.

Itsy Bitsy's mother said,
'Take care - and don't be late.
If Aunt Matilda isn't there,
come home and do not wait.'

Itsy Bitsy Missy Moo
plodded through the brook
and stood upon the hillside
to take a second look.

For stood by Aunt Matilda
beneath the cherry tree
was someone Itsy didn't know
and could not really see.

'Come see my brand new baby,'
Aunt Matilda proudly cried
and Itsy Bitsy Missy Moo
stood gently by her side.

And so you see, the best of friends
right to this very day,
are Itsy Bitsy Missy Moo
And Minnie Daisy-May!

Janice Mitchell

22nd May

The Guffalo

A creature quite remarkable,
Whose name gives you a clue,
He eats baked beans and sprouts all day
Then does a massive . . .

. . . pudding for his friends to consume.

Gazelle can't wait for this new treat,
Flamingo's tickled pink,
Giraffe and Zebra turn their nose
Up at his latest . . .

. . . stinging nettle shortcake surprise.

The guests are all excited now,
They wait with beating heart,
Lion and Monkey lick their lips
As he sneaks out a . . .

. . . family photograph album.

Crocodile wants to share his snaps,
Elephant trumps with glee,
Hippopotamus watches on
Whilst he begins to . . .

. . . weave a blanket to keep them warm.

Gorilla bangs and beats his chest,
Pelican starts to carp,
Snake and Ostrich demand a snack
So he does another . . .

. . . parmesan and pickle pasta.

Leopard and Cheetah still aren't full,
You'd think they'd had enough,
'Oh, I've got plenty left!' he cries
And lets rip one more . . .

. . . guffaw at Hyena's last joke.

Mark Paddington

23rd May

Moonsong For Tom

The buttery moon
climbed into the sky.
He slipped past the trees
then rode on high.

Up amongst the glittering stars
he smiled his moonish smile.
We stood on Earth and looked afar;
Oh Moon, dear Moon, you're many a mile.

Owls hooted and a fox crept by,
the dormouse opened his weary eye,
hens clucked and said, 'Not I,
you shall not have your chicken pie.'

The moon sailed on in the starry sky,
The world woke up and so did the boy.
He ran to the window and looked up high
but the moon had gone and he gave a sigh.

The very next night Tom looked at the sky.
The moon smiled down and winked his eye,
Tom smiled back, then climbed into bed.
'Thank you Moon,' was all he said.

Eileen Peggs

24th May

My Cheeky Computer

My computer usually does as it's told
whenever I hit the keys - but
one day it misbehaved, began writing
in Chinese

I didn't understand a word, so asked
a Chinese friend - who read
that my computer
said . . .

*You're driving me round the bend,
hitting my keys so carelessly;
I can't make sense of anything
you send!*

Cheeky! But now I spell more carefully,
my computer behaves perfectly

Roger N Taber

25th May

The Movement Beat

I keep running every day
Over hills and far away
Through the vales and up on high
Reaching out to touch the sky

Running over mountain tops
Bouncing over hop by hop
I'm shouting out, 'Here I come'
Calling out to everyone

Skipping, prancing through the streets
Everybody, keep the beat
Let everyone form a line
Dancing happy, all in time

Jumping up into the air
Wave your hands, like you don't care
Everybody, what's that noise
Happy, dancing girls and boys

Let the children say this beat
Jumping wildly, stamping feet
Singing to their hearts' content
Each new dance they will invent

Every path they choose to take
Makes them think and also wait
But no matter what they do
They'll keep helping me and you

Let them learn this brand new rhyme
Singing, moving, all in time
When their bodies start to ache
All sit down and have a break

Samuel Edwards

26th May

Little Bird

Little bird I saw you hit the high wire in my yard
You've passed it many times before, were you caught off guard?
As you fell and hit the ground, I watched your body lie
My little winter garden friend, I hoped you wouldn't die!
I first see you in autumn eating berries from the ground
A solitary figure among the other birds around
Your red breast can be seen as you move in flight
Darting from tree to tree, like a flash of light!
Just a ball of feathers, with tiny legs and wings
That brightens up the winter days with antics that he brings
Running to the scene below, felt like my heart would burst
With water to revive him and to quench his thirst
But when I reached the very spot, well what more can I say
My little friend had up and left - he had flown away!

Karl Jakobsen

27th May

Bedtime

Lay your sweet head down upon your bed,
Think of your day and what lies ahead.
Dreams I hope are happy and sweet,
All night long please don't peep!
A kiss I place softly on your face,
Gently stroking your hair back in place.
When tomorrow comes it shall be a new day,
Now that's all I must say,
Sleep tight, goodnight.

Zoe Fitzjohn

28th May

Growing Up

Hello?
Heelllloooo?
Where I am?
Someone, anyone, get me out of here! It's dark. *Whimper.*
Why I am wrapped up? Have I been kidnapped?
I feel weird. I feel . . . weird!
Grunt, grunt, wriggle, wriggle . . .
Ah! Daylight.
Pop!
What on earth are those on my head?
Where have my other legs gone?
What's happened to my body?
Prwhooosh!
Whoa! Wings! Cooooool!
I've got wings! Ha-ha! Wings! Brilliant!
. . . My wings are dry
Time to fly!

Off the butterfly flutters
Dancing to and fro
Off on adventures
To where? Who knows . . .

Courtney Marshall

29th May

Secret Place

At the bottom of my garden is a secret place
Where nobody goes but me
I go down into the garden after I've had my tea
You see past the pond and round the apple tree
Then down the stony path
You will see a big holly bush
And behind this there's a round door
You have to give it a little push
You see the door is only meant for little people like my secret friends
Who live inside
Do you know who they are?
I will give you some clues
They look like gnomes, they wear green outfits with hats with bells on
And little brown boots
They are the pixies
Nobody knows about them but me
We play and dance and giggle
Until to bed they go under a tree.

Crystal Waters

30th May

May

In the throes of May
We delight in going out to play
We dance round the maypole weaving ribbons over and under we go
The weather is warmer, spring is here
We all laugh and cheer
The birds sing their daily songs
As they gather food for their young
It's a wonderful time of year
We all love the springtime
The sun is out
The days are getting longer
We have no need for our winter coats
As we go outside and play in the sun
May is a great month
Lambs are being born
Farmers are planting their corn
All in all May is the greatest
A most lovely time of year
We are happy when May is here.

Heather Killingray

31st May

Minx The Manx Kitten

Minx the Manx kitten was once badly bitten
By the mischievous bug
She got mud on her paws, tiptoed indoors
Then walked up and down on the rug

Every fine morn, round about dawn
Minx waits on the doorstep for 'Milkie'
After he's been Minx steals the cream
To keep her fine coat soft and silky

One Tuesday in June, just about noon
Minx saw her first butterfly
She started a chase all over the place
And trampled the flowers, oh my!

The very next day Minx had to stay
Indoors, because of the weather
She jumped on the bed, unravelled a thread
And whoosh! caused a shower of feathers

Sometimes at night Minx gets a fright
When she goes for a walk before bed
There are squeaks in the eaves, rustles in leaves
And a toad with brown spots on its head

It should be understood, Minx tries to be good
But just when she thinks that she might
Her nose starts to itch, her whiskers to twitch
And she gets a strange buzz in that bite

Mary Younger

1st June

A Child's Thoughts

As I lie in bed, it's not quite dark
Children are still playing in the park.
If I peep round the curtain I might see
The bird that is singing in the tree.

If I was a bird then I would fly
Out of the window, up to the sky.
As I fly around, it will be dark soon
Then I can talk to the man in the moon.

The man in the moon must have lots of fun
As he looks down on everyone.
He is there all night, taking a peep
At all the people who are fast asleep.

He hears the owl hoot, and the wolf howl
He sees the animals out on the prowl.
The cat that creeps out of the house
Hoping to catch a tiny mouse.

When I grow up, I want to go
Up in a spaceship to say hello
To the man in the moon, who shines in my room
Chasing away the night-time gloom.

Lynne Walden

2nd June

The Legend Of Captain Blackwhiskers

You've heard some stories I am sure
Of *pirates* . . . tales are told
Of sailing on the seven seas
Hearts cold and courage bold

But settle down me hearties
For a secret yet unknown
There are terrifying pirate *cats*
News that's sure to chill your bones

Of all the famous pirate ships
The most feared is the Golden Claw
Aboard, a crew of miscreants
Defying Admiralty Law

Blackwhiskers is their Captain
A truly fearsome cat
Braids weaved into his matted fur
And fish bones in his hat

His mission always is the same
To hunt for hidden treasures
And to instil fear and horror
With no room for half measures

So if you are out sailing
And on the horizon you do spy
A black ship with a flag of fish bones
Hoisted high into the sky

Feel fear, for you must flee
You will need to sail fast and far
Or you will become the latest
To hear Blackwhiskers growl 'Ha! Har!.'

Alison Pickard

3rd June

Dance Of The Fairies

To and fro they wave at me so,
Flickering, frightening consume where they go,
Crackling, cackling they mock me at night
Preying on my nerves, tickling my fright.

Rising and falling or murmuring low,
Would dance on me too, this I do know.
Disregarding all to them it is nought
Anything but water they don't spare a thought.

But, me they want; I hear it in their whispers
In the night, *especially* in the night's strange vistas,
Their flittering shadows on me they throw,
Dance on in my eyes, while their embers lay low.

T J Shaw

4th June

Incy Wincy Spider

Incy wincy spider scuttled across the floor
On came the light so he bolted for the door
This time it seemed, he surely had been seen
If he were caught, they would treat him really mean.
Incy wincy spider didn't want this fate
Quick as a flash he climbed onto a plate
Spied a swarm of flies eating all the crumbs
Swallowed them down just like juicy plumbs.
Incy wincy spider, so full he couldn't climb
Lay down his head and regretted his crime.
Along came the master, whispered, 'Clever you'
The spider smiled then disappeared from view.

Kathleen Potter

5th June

Reg Rabbit

Have you seen Reg Rabbit
When he goes out for tea?
He really looks ridiculous
And stupid as can be!
He wears a bonnet on his head
With flowers of red and blue,
A long white dress of frilly lace
With bows of every hue
His socks are green and purple
With little dots of red
His shoes are long black booties
With laces to his head.
Beads of every colour
Are dangling from his ears,
When I saw him dancing
I was reduced to tears.

Have you seen Reg Rabbit
When he goes out to tea?
He really looks ridiculous
And stupid as can be.

Peggy Briston

6th June

Let's Go

My puppy dog, big ears, long nose,
Snappy, go - fetch the stick.
We run in the park, the cool wind blows,
I can't keep up, you're too quick.

Watch out! Your paws will make a mess,
Their picnic was nice, what did you do?
I'm sorry Sir, it wasn't me, I confess.
Do you know who the mutt belongs to?

He's really friendly and gentle and nice,
He wouldn't even harm a flea.
Once I saw him cuddle with mice
And even helped a cat down from a tree.

Come here boy, never leave me alone,
Let's be on our way, let's go home.

Lee A Marsh

7th June

Farts

Farts and trumps are so much fun
I like the silent deadly one
It's better when the classroom's quiet
I let one rip and cause a riot!

Mom never does it, it's funny that
She always seems to blame the cat!
If we do it in company, Mom will moan
Telling us off for 'lowering the tone'.

When our dogs do it, it's so much fun
They always spin round and stare at their bum!
Our baby nephew is only a learner
Until he grows up to be chief botty burner!

Last year at Christmas, we remember so well
Our dad had produced a very bad smell
He's got hidden talents, he can fart in time
To the whole of the chorus of 'Auld Lang Syne'!

If we go in Dad's bedroom, it's not so appealing
To find all the bedclothes an inch from the ceiling!
We put on a *gas mask* and hand him his toast
And pray we don't have to come back with his post!

Isn't it strange how farts are such fun
A peculiar sound that comes from your bum
Everyone does it, except for the Queen,
Well maybe, that remains to be seen!

Julie Trainor

8th June

Lira The Cat

The cat, it liked to tease the mouse
So food it did but chew
The cat kept some food in its mouth
But the mouse already knew

The cat sat still and did but wait
Till the mouse smelled the aroma
The mouse appeared, all but too late
The cat was asleep in a coma

The mouse did laugh as food did seep
From the sly cat's little grin
The mouse was fed as the cat did sleep
And the mouse kissed the cat on the chin.

Charlotte McMullen

9th June

Some Day

Once in a meadow,
a long time ago,
there lived a small bunny
who could only hop, slow.

When all the young bunnies
would race through the grass,
this one little bunny
would always be last.

He spoke to his father -
'cause he wanted to know
if the rest of his life
he would always be slow?

'Never give up, Son,'
his father would say.
'Try to be patient
you will make it someday.

Just keep on believing
and someday you'll see
that when it's your time
you'll be just like me.'

As spring changed to summer
the bunny did too grow,
and soon he discovered
he no longer was slow.

That small little bunny
who was last for so long
had grown to a rabbit -
steady and strong.

9th June

Now when they gather
to race in the grass,
nobody can catch him
because he's too fast!

And he always remembers
when his father would say,
'Never give up, Son,
you will make it someday.'

Tom Krause

10th June

Mrs Back To Front

Goodbye, goodbye! I'd hear her say
Whenever people passed her way.

It wasn't 'cause she was too blunt
It was because she's back to front.

People laughed as she walked by
She'd turn and smile and know not why.

They would point and they would stare
She would smile and have no care.

Her clothes you see, were on the wrong way
She never knew if it was night or day.

Her clocks ticked left - instead of right,
Her cooking turned out a terrible sight.

She liked to ride upon her horse
Along the street, the wrong way of course.

She faced his bottom instead of his head
She's in a muddle, the town folk said.

Hello, hello she's off somewhere
Clothes back to front and not a care.

Denise Pettitt (Children's Entertainer)

 11th June

Dinosaur's Feast

Urns of slime
and reptiles' heads
giants' feet
and mouldy breads

Icy hearts
and mountain eggs
a ton of tongues
and turtle legs

Frogs and beetles
chewed to gristle
old pine cones
all spiced with thistle

Snake-flesh paste
and baby whales
slowly stirred
with heads and tails

Fishes' eyes
and insects' skin
mixed and mixed
till thick and thin

All gulped down
with spidery glue
which sleepy dinosaurs
forget to chew

Katherine Gallagher

12th June

The Sea-Less Sea Of Fishes

In a magical land where no one dares to wish, is the sea-less sea
of fishes made up of mostly . . . fish,
Elephant's trunks, alien's toes and little blue sherbet mermaids.
In this place, nothing grows.
For no earth or mud or grass is here, only carpet - plain, patterned and cashmere.
For when King Stupid reigned the land, he had the entire floor carpeted by hand,
And so he ordered his army of bees to pull up the trees and flowers
(or he said he'd break their knees).
But now the king was long since gone, Queen Wonderful had cut off his head.
'We must right the wrongs, of which there are many, we are better off now he's dead.
He bathed in noodles and sang out of tune, he shouted at pixies and
was afraid of the moon.
He sent all the chickens to work down the mines and all people with
beards were made to pay fines.
For the sea is shrinking into the ground, sea monsters for once
are not making a sound.
The sea is crying and dying and lying so low, that it cannot be found.
These carpets are stupid, they soak and they squelch, they munch
and they crunch and they roar and they belch.
All of nature is dying and we must act fast, if not all this beauty
which surrounds us, won't last.'
The Queen upon hearing of this stupid man, set to work spreading
the news of his evil plan -
'We will overthrow and under-jump, we will save the sealife and call his trump.'
It was easy to say and easy to do, she presented the king with a
present for *'you-hoo!'*
She cooed and she fluttered her fingers at the cat, then she struck
with a wallop and a mighty big splat.
His head rolled away down the corridor, the Queen put the axe
down upon the floor,
'Prepare the vessel and brew the jam tea, we must set sail at once
or at least by about three?'
Her plan was not simple, her plan was not clear but she knew
of a wizard, one of magic and fear.

12th June

This wizard he grew by the size and the load, great
monsters of all colours, shapes and abode.
So she bargained and bartered and screamed and cried,
to negotiate with him but he wanted a bride.
'Never!' she cried, 'I will cut off your head!'
'You can try,' the wizard smiled, 'but I am already dead!'
As she swept from the castle a voice by her side squeaked,
'We want to leave, can you please help us try?'
'If you can eat carpet by day and by night and help rid the world of
its horrible plight, then my promise from me to you will be this,
the wizard will be gone and you will lead a life of pure bliss.'
The monsters all squeaked and under Queenie's bright eye, started
eating the floor as if it were cherry pie.
Queen stood before Wizard and said with a grin,
'I agree to your terms, you're aware I live in a bin?
I've taken your monsters they're chewing the floor -
soon the sea will return and this drought will be no more.'
The wizard turned scarlet-red in the face, pinched his nose and said,
'You may leave now, Your Grace.'

Kerrie Wood

13th June

Sleepy Princess Niddy

Once upon a time in a land far far away
There lived a sleepy princess with long hair
No, she wasn't Sleeping Beauty or even Rapunzel
But she was definitely halfway there.

The little princess who's name was Niddy
Was sat at the window in a daze
She needed to rescue the kingdom from darkness
And she just had a couple of days!

Three nights ago she sat eating, up a tree
When she dropped her big silver spoon
It hit her pet, Daisy, who went a little crazy
And that cow ran away with the moon!

Since then it had been dark in the kingdom
Without the moon, there had been no light
Poor Niddy had to think of what to do
To bring back the moon that night.

Eureka! Niddy jumped up with a bright idea
And tried to show it to her jester called Jake
But the jester had to keep blowing the trumpet
To keep the sleepy princess awake!

With binoculars she ran up to the window
And threw the fishing rod as far as she could
She didn't know how but it had skipped over the cow
And hooked the moon, like she knew that it would!

So Niddy reeled the moon to high up in the sky
And the future was no longer bleak
And since then there has been light at night
And Princess Niddy's been fast asleep.

Sabreena Hussain

 14th June

The Trouble With Parents Is . . .

They nag and shout,
They moan and tease,
They keep secrets
    - like a conspiracy,
And they talk about me!

They stay up all night
And at home all day.
They make plans
    behind my back
And always get the
    wrong end of the stick.

They're always talking,
They think they know everything
And they tell you
    not to do something
Then they do it themselves!

Josephine Reading

15th June

Harry Hare

Harry the hare was so full of starch,
Because it was the month of March,
A time when hares run wild and free,
As fast - as fast - as fast as can be!

Harry zigzagged swiftly to and fro,
Not really knowing which way to go,
Back and forth he frantically ran,
As fast - as fast - as fast as he can!

Harry the hare scampered far and wide,
In leaps and bounds over the countryside,
On and on and through a fern-filled wood,
As fast - as fast - as fast as he could!

Harry the hare now quickened his pace,
Briskly darting all over the place,
March time madness was even greater fun,
The faster - the faster - Harry did run!

T D Green

16th June

The King's Crown

Black clouds hung over King George's life
bringing howling winds of despair,
sadness wrapped his heart in chains
as his thoughts played solitaire.

His golden crown was missing jewels
of happiness, love and care,
his former queen had taken them
and left misery everywhere.

Sarah, his most trusted servant
confidant and friend,
staked a claim to break the chains
and save the King from a bitter end.

She sent a message to the High Powers
inscribed in a candle's flame,
requesting they replace the missing jewels
and send a new queen to share his name.

The Powers replied, disguised as a dream
that her wish would soon be granted,
love would return, tenfold to the King
and the seeds were already planted.

The sun broke through as the new queen arrived
turning his tears into love and laughter,
she placed a new crown upon his head
and they lived happily ever after.

Jan Janik

17th June

Dad's Snoring

My dad snores, oh boy, how he snores!
He sounds just like a timber yard with huge buzz-saws.

Mum tried hard to cure him,
First she sewed a tennis ball
Into the back of his pyjamas
That did no good at all.

And Dad still snores, brother how he snores!
He rumbles like a jungle full of hungry lions' roars.

Mum's friend, Marie, suggested
She tried electric shock,
Dad's hair all stood up on end
But his nose stayed just as blocked.

So Dad still snores, crikey how he snores!
It sounds as if an earthquake is rattling the doors.

Mum built a lifter-roller
To turn Dad on his side
His snoring just got louder
She cried and cried and cried.

And still Dad snores, golly how he snores!
It's louder than the football when the home team scores.

At last Mum talked to Grandma
Now everything's alright,
Gran told Mum the secret
Of peaceful sleep at night.

Oh Dad still snores, but now nobody hears;
We bought a bale of cottonwool to stuff into our ears!

Joy Green

18th June

Flutter By

There was a tree on the edge of a wood
Where upon a leaf, a butterfly stood
Wings open wide, all her colours on show
She was trying to decide which way to go.
Her wings were of orange, red and blue
And around the edge there was a hue
Of yellowish-green, black and white
They really were a magnificent sight.

Rising up on her toes she's ready for flight
Flapping her wings with all her might
Until she flutters up into the sky
Up, up, so very high.
Swirling, twirling round and round
Then delicately flying back down to the ground
Along in the breeze we see her glide,
Into a bush and out the other side.

Now she has gone way beyond our sight
Looking for a shelter to rest for the night
The question we ask is, 'Where did she go?'
The answer to that we'll never know.
Do not be sad, there is no sorrow
As we shall see her tomorrow
For once again, she'll flutter by
Our beautiful butterfly.

Nicola Hopkins

19th June

Animal Antics Part 1

Benjamin's dad called out, 'Ben, time for bed,
tidy your room, Mum'll come up soon.'
Ben climbed the stairs and brushed his teeth,
lay down on his bed and fell fast asleep.

A big baboon tiptoed in, is Benjamin asleep?
Two giraffes at the window, took a little peep.
A chimpanzee zipped down the window blind
to the beating drums from a gorilla, with a big behind.
Tum-te-tum . . . dum-de-dum.

A koala played calmly with a squeaky crane.
An orang-utan tried to ride the toy train.
A kangaroo hopped in with a picnic, looking glum,
as the laughing hyena raced over and ate all the plums.

Benjamin stirred from his sleep,
rubbed his eyes and dared to peep.
He heard a strange noise and went to explore,
and quietly opened the bathroom door.

Three buffaloes were squashed in the bathroom.
Four lizards danced on the loo.
Alligators aired in the drying cupboard,
and some hippos hid in there too!

Turtles paddled on the sink top,
an elephant flopped in the bath,
a snake curled around the shower tap,
and Benjamin began to laugh.

Meanwhile, a mongoose stretched on the sofa,
with a tiger, watching TV.
A leopard sprawled in the armchair
with an Emu on his knee.

19th June

A zebra strolled in with his backpack, all neat,
emptied it out and began to eat.
A lion prowled around the peaceful group,
and ordered like a king . . . 'I'd like some tomato soup.'

But just as Ben stirred again in his sleep,
he heard his mum's steps on the stairs.
'Oh dear,' he whispered, 'What can I do?
She'll find all the animals, just escaped from the zoo.'

Gillian Hesketh

20th June

Gregory And Tess

My mum and dad are both mad at me!
At me! Yes me!
Young Gregory!
And it's all because of the fuss over Tess
and the tin of paint by the tree.

I just wanted to show her a colour
cos Dad told me cats only see
in black and white.
Well, me being Gregory
I don't think that's right,
so I decided to show her a colour
or maybe two.

It wasn't my fault
she scratched and she fought
as I held her by the tail
over the tin
cos if she hadn't
she wouldn't have fallen in!

When Mum and Dad
saw that Tess
was a blue mess
they became red
and sent me to my room
and to my bed!

From my window I spied them
washing Tess with soap and a brush
and it was all done in such a rush
so that the paint wouldn't dry.

Now I can see that Tess is
once again a tabby
and if you ask me I think
she looks rather shabby
and was better off being a bit blue.

But I'd better not tell that to my mum and dad
who're asking me
young Gregory
to come and get my tea!

Brian McInally

21st June

Night Vs Day

The sun and the moon had a quarrel.
Said the sun, 'I am greater than you!'
The moon disagreed and said softly,
'I'm sorry that's simply not true,
for where would we be without moonbeams
to light up the traveller's path?
And what would they do when it's cloudy?'
The sun simply said, 'That's a laugh!
Without any sun, there'd be darkness.
It also would be very cold.
No flowers would bloom without sunshine,
no trees would live long and grow old.'
The quarrel went on for a long time,
it seemed they just could not agree
so they asked Mother Nature what she thought.
She said, 'Now you listen to me.
The sun lights the day. The moon lights the night.
It's really as simple as that.
Each one means as much as the other.
Now let's put an end to this spat!'
The sun and the moon nodded sweetly,
decided that she must be right.
The sun wins the race every morning.
The moon wins the race every night.

J P Henderson-Long

22nd June

The Search

If you swing north-east
And bypass plains and mountains,
And stop for neither bird nor man nor beast,
Then walk straight on across the icy tundra
And join no tribe in sacrificial feast,
You will come at last with mounting jubilation
And a pleasure that is really quite absurd,
To the hidden sacred nesting habitation,
Of the spotted cross-billed Giggelhymer bird,
The splendid spotted Giggelhymer bird.

He nests upon a raft right in the river
All hung about and hidden from the view,
It has bells around the entrance which all jangle,
To tell him if a stranger comes - like you.
But do not try to snare him with a bangle,
Or yet a tie pin or a tasty yam,
For he won't be caught by any piece of twangle,
Or a sandwich made of someone's yummy jam,
No not even for a sandwich made of jam.

So sit and think before you go a-hunting,
Do you really wish the Giggelhyme to snatch?
No, try some other form of expeditious stalking,
But do not try this splendid bird to catch.
This very special splendid bird to catch.

D M Neu

23rd June

The Mighty Snore

The bird in the tree
flew down to see
if the fish in the lake was awake,
'Of course I'm awake,'
he said, munching some cake
'but for goodness sake
who is that snoring?'

The fish and the bird
had a private word
then went at a jog and found the frog,
but silent was Frog
catching flies on a log,
'Try the dog,' he croaked
'he finds life boring.'

But the dog was awake,
he was eating a steak,
far too busy to let out a snore,
'Not me,' he said,
'I'm not even in bed!
have you checked out
the cat next door?'

'That deafening noise?'
purred the cat, 'It's the boys.'
But the boys said, 'Don't get in a paddy!
We know that snore,
we have heard it before,
it's the mighty snore
of our Daddy!'

Valerie Sutton

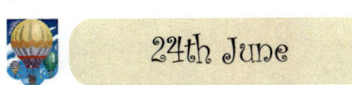

24th June

Julian The Hooligan

Julian the hooligan was only five years old,
He bashed and smashed and shouted and wouldn't do as he was told.
He scratched and snatched and hatched out plans for naughty things to do
And if he ever saw a ghost you can bet that he'd say *boo!*

Beneath his bed a creature lay, all teeth and slimy scales,
And in the day it hid away from Julian's awful wails.
It would squeeze its yellow eyes tight shut and hold its breath in fear
And tremble in its scaly skin at the sounds that it could hear.

At night the creature lay quite still and tried hard not to shake,
He'd listen to Julian breathe, afraid that he might wake.
One night it sighed a sorrow-filled sigh and with a sniff it said;
'I wish my dad was here to clear the monster from over my bed!'

Abigail Cowley

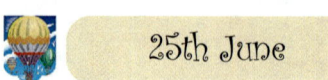

25th June

Tree Rings In My Poem

I'm going to write some words today,
My pencil is coloured red,
Some words are on the blackboard,
'Write a poem,' the teacher said.

I grasp the pencil firmly,
I start the word called 'trees',
The next word is an 'are' word
Then, 'very', then 'old' then 'these'.

Trees are very old, I write,
These rings mark out its time.
I'll have to have a rest now
Because the next lines have to rhyme.

I wonder if my grandad
Has lines inside him too?
They must be crushed together,
He's nearly eighty-two.

Trees stand against the frost and rain
They're satisfied with their lot,
Like grandma when she's talking
Of the life she'd not forgot.

So when you sit beneath a tree,
Listen, let it sing
Its melody, a story
Of summer, winter, spring.

Gerard Melia

26th June

The Moon

Crescent at first sight,
Slowly you come in the night
But day after day you grow up
As a baby tends to grow.

You light the Earth
When you're full at night,
Shaped like my basketball
I played in the game hall.

You're a blessing for the Earth
You brighten also the night
Aided with stars that glow
And globe the Earth, whenever you blow.

Aderemi Adegbite

27th June

Faraway Dreams

It's time to sleep
so close your eyes
tuck in ted and
snuggle up tight

The stars above
shining on you
sand man wishing
you sweet dreams too

Dream about a
faraway place
wondrous things in
front of your face

A sea so blue,
a sand so white,
glistening from
the bright sunlight

Brightly lit trees
covered in fruit
dazzling in
their colours true

Stay 'til morning
lie in the sand
until next time
you visit that land

Paola Borella

28th June

The Miserable Dragon

Daniel was a dragon with a blocked-up nose,
He was miserable down to the tips of his toes.

Daniel was brave, he was tall, he was proud
And normally he'd been exceedingly loud.
But instead of a roar and a hot burst of flame,
Only a stuffy kind of fizzy squeak came!
Daniel tried mixtures and sweets that you suck,
But whatever he tried, he had no luck.

Daniel was gloomy and felt so blue,
He really didn't know what to do.

Blowing his nose with a ginormous handkerchief,
Made his nose red and brought him no relief.
Daniel couldn't even fly through the air -
It made his ears pop so much he didn't dare.
He stood on his head, which for dragons isn't easy,
But that didn't clear his head, it just made him queasy!

Daniel was snotty and sniffy and really glum,
His stuffed-up state was extremely tiresome.

Daniel called on a friend to seek his aid -
By the hot springs where billowing steam was made.
Daniel sat hunched in his miserable state
Unaware that the steam was changing his fate.
His head started clearing - his snottiness too,
He jumped up smiling, his nose felt like new.

He sniffed and he snorted and gave a great shout -
He was breathing air in and whooshing flames out!
Daniel was so happy, he soared into the sky
And bellowing fire and smoke, he flew higher than high.

Glenys Chapman

29th June

Summer Fun

My face, it's moving . . .
My eyes are getting *big* . . .
My cheeks are s-t-r-e-t-c-h-i-n-g . . .
I've turned my frown upside down
Summer's here
My grin's from ear to ear!
Hooray for l-o-n-g sunny days
Ice cream and paddling pools
Holidays that amaze
And no more *school!*
(Well, just for a little while, but it still makes me s   e!
                                                                     m i l

Sparkle Andrews

 30th June

Gilly The Giraffe

Gilly the giraffe was very, very small
Apart from her neck that was quite, quite tall
Her mum and her dad said that she would grow
But Gilly thought, *that can't be so.*

One day on a cold and frosty night
The stars came out very bright
Gilly awoke and saw the moon
It shone in her window until Mum sang her tune

Gilly the giraffe ran out of bed
Smelling the eggs cooking in the shed
She glanced in the mirror and then she saw
Gilly had grown more, more, more!

Megan Wileman (12)

1st July

Smile Children

One day a smile I wore had grown
too big for one small child to own,
and so I gave up half of it
to someone else. It seemed to fit,
but it too then began to grow,
till half of that smile had to go.

Soon smiles were being passed about
like candy - yes, I have no doubt
my smile and all its children now
are everywhere! It's funny how
one smile can do so much. It's true.
Why, look - it's made its way to *you*.

Rich Roach

2nd July

High Up In The Corner

High up in the corner
Of my sister's and my room
Lives a black and hairy spider
In the corner, in the gloom.
His eyes are bright and beady
His legs are rather long
He looks a little clumsy
But he's nimble and he's strong.
I don't mind him being there
In the middle of his web
'Cause when I see him there, at home
He'll not be in my bed.
But one day he looked bigger
Than he had the day before
My little sister cried and said,
'I don't like him anymore.'
So Mummy said she'd sort it
And took the vacuum to our room
To suck him from the corner
Or hit him with the broom.
I think he's very clever
And his hearing awfully good
He must have heard Mum coming
And he'd scarpered while he could.
The next morning in the corner
I spied him hanging there
And I'm sure I saw him wave at me
From his corner, on the stair.

Lisa Oldham

3rd July

Enormous Norman

Enormous Norman was normally slow,
So gross was his body he just couldn't go
Any faster than snails' pace, which as you all know
Is almost as slow as the glaciers flow.

The whole of his bulk he would lean to one side,
Then from deep down below, one foot he would slide
A little way forward, before he then tried
With the other to follow it in a slow glide.

To watch Norman move was a wondrous sight.
To get to his bed would take him all night,
Then as morning appeared he'd use all of his might
To raise his prepond'rance to posture upright

But if he should chance to be close to some food,
On anyone's party he'd simply intrude.
His antics right then would appear to be rude
As he elbowed his way through anyone's brood.

His hands would move swift as a centipede runs,
To fill up his face with the best of the buns
Or cream cakes or chocolates or packets of gums.
He'd demolish the lot and not even leave crumbs!

But as a result of his speed and his greed,
He departed this life in the midst of a feed
When he ruptured his gut, taking more than he need,
He exploded and scattered like dandelion seed.

Barbara Lucy Hosken

4th July

Lullaby

Little darling, please don't cry
Mama's gonna sing you a lullaby
No need for you to cry or weep
Time for you to go to sleep

If you close your tired eyes
You can see how the pixie flies
See the man in the moon on a white moonbeam
Have lots of adventures in your dream

If you try to fall asleep
You can dream of the sea so deep
Of mermaids playing in the waves
And treasure in the dolphins' caves

In a dream there is no place you can't go
Visit Santa Claus in the Arctic snows
Go to Toyland to see Mr Teddy Bear
Tell a dragon to fly with you through the air

If something tries to frighten you
Tell them 'Off and away with you!'
All you have to do is call
Papa will come and chase you all

I promise you that when you wake
At the very first sound you make
I will pick you up and hold you tight
And let in the new morning light

Little darling, please don't cry
Mama's gonna sing you a lullaby . . .

Daniela Schwarz

5th July

Morning, Noon And Night

early in the morning
just as it gets light
Mr Pippin goes to work
on his motorbike

breakfast at last
at quarter-past nine
marmalade and toast
yummy, that's fine

dinner time arrives
at twelve o'clock noon
a nice bowl of soup
with his favourite spoon

then he opens his lunch box
and takes out a slice
of cherry tart cake
yummy that's nice

now back to work
till half-past four
and then home for dinner
he's hungry for sure

sausage and mash
on a nice bed of beans
a large crust of bread - *hmm*
- the dish of his dreams

now a warm bath
nearly time for bed
Mr Pippin goes to sleep
with a tummy that's well fed

David Chapman

6th July

The Dove

The dove sat on the wooden fence,
It did not move a muscle,
It saw the cats come from the path,
And watched them in their tussle.
The dove felt it was lucky,
That the cats did not espy,
Its little bod upon the fence,
Before it off did fly.

M Wilcox

7th July

Tigger And Floppy

Tigger is the nickname
Of a big black cat
And Floppy is the name
Of an old sheepdog
Who both live together
In Crowbank Hall
Which stands so proudly
In Oakridge Woods

Both good friends
Like to chase one another
Through the trees and shrubs
Of those beautiful woods
Then into the wide open spaces beyond
Where they can run and play
Until the end of day
When the golden sun goes down

Donald John Tye

8th July

Joy Supreme

You are the light
That illuminates my soul
You are my insight
And instant joy to extol.

The twinkle of stars
I feel in your warm embrace
All the future fears
With your innocence, erase.

Serenity and refinement
I glimpse in your vivid eyes
Darkness flies afar in heart
Paving way for surprise.

Life entwined with life
Shared with trust and sacrifice
Let it either be joy or grief
I shall bury with your fond face.

Whenever you play with toys
A shining pearl, likewise you plunge
Into the deep sea of my joys
Exciting me with a passionate rage.

The striking rainbow in the sky
Is visible in your serene smile
I conserve it as a supreme joy
To cross life, mile after mile.

Tholana Ashok Chakravarthy

9th July

Ode Spider, Ode Spider, What Did You Do?

A tiny,
Black old spider,
Was sitting,
On the drive.

When the rain,
Began to fall,
He made a dash,
Inside.

Into the porch,
Then out the back,
And halfway,
Up a wall.

There he found,
A biggish hole,
Which tripped,
And made him fall.

Into space,
He made his drop,
His eyes,
He shut up tight.

But when,
He hit the solid ground,
He splattered
Like a kite.

9th July

So the spider,
Passed away,
No more
To sit in rain.

The only thing,
He'd ever done,
Was give,
Miss Muffet fame.

Alvin Creighton

10th July

Horizons – A Child's View

At four years of age I painted the sky
High up at the top of the paper.
I painted it there at the top very high
And the grass at the bottom came later.

My brother was scornful, asking me why,
And what did I think was between there?
I said there was nothing between earth and sky
Except, everyone knew, there was 'clear air'.

He said, 'No!' - they met a long way away
And that it was called the horizon;
So I was a silly to think in my way
And he knew because he was the wise one.

One day at the table, he asked about bread
And what did Dad think it was made of?
'That's easy enough,' I quietly said,
For, my brother I was not afraid of.

Quite nonchalantly I twiddled my thumbs:
'Well, what is it then?' he demanded.
'If you really must know, it is made out of crumbs,'
I said, thinking him quite reprimanded.

'Crumbs?' he laughed. 'Crumbs!' - and I couldn't think why
He could not see what was so easy;
But in that he thought that the earth met the sky,
It seemed quite plain to me he was crazy.

E Marjorie Bright

11th July

A Cautionary Tale

Horace Hillman had a hamster
Holding Hammy in his hand
Did a handstand in the playground
Hammy didn't understand!

Betty Button picked him up
And put him quickly in her bag
Went to clean the classroom windows
Used poor Hammy as a rag!

Charlie Clifford saw poor Hammy
Wet and shaking on the floor
Went and put him in his pocket
Hit his head upon the door.

In came, Mr Clarke, the teacher,
'Sit down Class,' he gruffly said.
Saw poor Hammy by the doorway
Mistook him for a hamster . . . *dead!*

Horace, Betty, Charlie, Teacher
Looked upon him with surprise
When he *twitched* his little whiskers
Ran away before their eyes.

Horace, Betty, Charlie Clifford
Feeling sad because he'd gone
Quietly went about their work
Feeling that there was no fun.

Suddenly the teacher called them,
'Horace, Betty, children, *look*
Can you see there by the window
Hammy sitting on that book.

Back into his cage they put him
Fed him till his cheeks grew fat
Pets need looking after always
So children please remember that.

Ruth Clark

12th July

The Cleaner

A cinema, a dark old place
Where kids can go to feed their face
And watch a film or maybe two
But something's there, it's watching you.

And when you're munching on your sweets
Sitting with your bag of treats
And you have chocolate round your chops
Some ice cream, a can of fizzy pops
Have you ever wondered where
The rubbish goes beneath your chair
And who cleans up when you're not there?

The film it ends, you leave your seat
The cinema does not look neat
It's full of bags and sticky things
It's gross, it smells of onion rings
Then who pops out and takes a sniff
A 'cleaner' who just loves the whiff
But does he clean, oh no not likely
He eats the mess so fast and sprightly.

The cleaner runs around the aisles
Just like a goblin, he never smiles
He's short, he's fat, he smells of wee
He's really not my cup of tea
His face is red from all the food
He's eaten, he is very rude
But is there more than just this one
There's too much food for just one tum.

No, many more come crawling out
They run around, they scream and shout
They munch, they crunch, they gorge their face
They think they're in an eating race
And in the blink of just one eye
The cinema is eaten dry
It's clean again, it smells no more

12th July

And there's no rubbish left on the floor.
So next time when you're in the chair
Of a cinema, think who is there
The cleaner waits with face so red
And while you're sleeping in your bed
He's eating all the food left there
The food you left beneath your chair.

Andy Wheeler

13th July

The Chimpanzee

It's fun to watch the chimpanzee,
Long arms stretching from tree to tree.
Impish monkeys running wild,
Eating everything they find.
Nuts and treats and sweet banana,
Fits in well with their persona.
Laughing, jumping in the air,
I saw one smack his derriere!
Children laugh and squeal with glee
As they count them - one, two, three.

Monkeys play such naughty tricks,
Tossing straw and throwing sticks.
If you mimic what they do,
They throw banana skins at you.
Sometimes they will pull your hair,
If you laugh at them and stare.
Sometimes they are very good,
Behaving like they know they should.
Almost human, just like you,
Though, please don't copy what they do!

Joyce Graham

14th July

Jam Sandwiches, Please

Is it hiding in your wardrobe
Or lurking beneath your bed?
Is your monster really there
Or just living in your head?
Perhaps your monster is cuddly
To snuggle up in bed,
Or is it a ferocious beast
Who might bite off your head?
Does it like to eat jam sandwiches
When invited out for tea?
Is your monster vegetarian,
Or will it take a bite off from me?

Hazel Calpee

15th July

Roseanna

In those days long ago, near a lake far away,
Lived a gentle white duck named Roseanna.
She had bright orange feet and a dark yellow bill
And her eyes were the colour of amber.
Yes, her eyes were the colour of amber.

But, Roseanna, she was an unhappy young duck,
She just sat on the beach broken-hearted,
While her brothers and sisters had fun on the lake,
For Roseanna was scared of the water,
That poor duck was so scared of the water!

One fine day a young lady came down to the lake,
There to feed the ducks biscuits and breadcrumbs.
When her basket was empty the lady went home.
She went home, but she left her umbrella.
Yes, the lady forgot her umbrella.

Our Roseanna quacked loud, 'Now I know what to do
For umbrellas will float on the water.
All I need is an old plastic bag as a sail,
And a sunflower leaf as a rudder.
A big sunflower leaf as a rudder.'

So she sailed her umbrella-ship out on the lake,
Where she played with her brothers and sisters.
'Now my feet will stay dry!' Roseanna quacked loud,
And she happily sailed ever after.
Oh, Roseanna sailed happily after.

Leo Cappel

15th July

16th July

Peter Brown At Billy Smart's Circus

Peter Brown said to the clown,
'Oh what a funny face you have,
With a red, large nose and a funny smile,
With your eyes painted with make-up.

Like golden blue stars,
With your hair matted and curled,
Sporting a large pointed hat,
And your long feet coloured in black.

Oh please do not frown when you're called into the circus ring,
Where a hundred children wait so patiently for you to sing,
For the fun to begin as the flour and water falls from your pail,
And you clap so loudly when you fall over the rail.'

'Yes,' said the clown to Peter Brown,
'The circus is fun when being a clown,
As you entertain the happy crowd
Here in Lutterworth market town.

With so many balls, I juggle them high,
While I skip and jump so freely,
That I duck and dive as all the children come alive,
It's then that I distort my face with a funny smile.

And I stick out my red, fat tongue,
While I squeeze a water gun in retaliation for the noise,
With my black and white harlequin clothes,
That are large, baggy and glum,

While I walk, fall, race and run,
Somersaulting backwards where a lion roars,
Who kicks red sand all over the place,
Straight into a large water bucket,

16th July

That sends it flying into space,
That I fall off my donkey called Fred,
Who rears its ugly head
For a showdown at Billy Smart's Circus.'

When one silly kid runs out,
Smirking all over his face,
'Yes,' said Peter Brown to the clown.

James S Cameron

17th July

Pixies And Fairies

The room is now dark and goodnight has been said,
my big brother and I are both tucked up in bed.

What Mum doesn't know as she turns out the light,
is the land that we visit together each night.

The pixies are there and the fairies are too,
only we can confront them and that's what we do.

There's wee pixie Billy and big fairy George,
and through all our meetings a friendship's been forged.

Our nights are exciting and no one knows why,
they don't know we visit our friends in the sky.

Their land is so happy, we laugh all the time,
as we play together we tumble and climb.

This land is our secret that no one else knows,
for if they knew of it they'd all want to go.

But come the bright morning our playmates have gone,
they're all sound asleep now as we sing their song.

Patsy Goodsir

18th July

The Mice

'Run to the hills,' little Mouse cried,
'I see a kestrel, let's go and hide.'
Straight up the hill they scurried fast,
Right to the top until at last
They took their rest till night-time drew,
When over their heads Tawny Owl flew.

'Run down the hill!' little Mouse cried,
'Into a valley, let's go and hide.'
Straight down the hill they scurried fast,
Right to the bottom until at last
They took their rest till daytime drew,
But were they safe? If only they knew!

When morning came they were in fact
In a garden with the neighbourhood cat.
'Stop!' said tiny Mouse. 'Wait right here,
We need to stop and face our fears.'
The mice stood still and huddled close,
Facing who they feared the most.

'Dinner, Puss Cat!' someone called.
Puss Cat turned to jump the wall.
'Shh!' whispered tiny Mouse. 'There he goes.'
With a sigh of relief and a twitch of his nose.
'Hooray!' they shouted. 'We are saved.
Thanks to tiny Mouse we were brave.'

Deborah Hall

19th July

Witch Way For India

'I can't spell, I won't spell!' India screamed one day.
Her teacher stood in silence - looked and waited.
'Now put your hat on straight and we'll start again,'
Her teacher said quietly, with a smile.
'Now sit up straight and repeat these rhymes after me . . .
I before E, except after C . . .'
And so the class went on, and on, and on, and on . . .
Soon India was fast asleep, her hat firmly over her eyes.

A sudden rapping on the lectern and the heavy thud
Of a book closing brought India back to life.
'You come from a long line of witches, India,
Your great aunt was a great spellist.
If she sez that once more, India thought, through gritted teeth,
*I'll set my broomstick upon her. Well I would I if could.
How many Zs in a spell that would make a teacher disappear?*
She plotted - sadly not enough, I fear.

Soon and not too soon, India left Rookery Grange School,
Sadly never made it to a fully-fledged witch,
But did achieve A-plus in broomstick skills and
As you can guess, D-minus in spell-casting.
But not all is lost - India is now making her own magic,
Quite satisfactory and happy, she became
An illustrator of children's books!

David Charles

20th July

When I'm A Man

When I am a grown man, I shall sail the seven seas
Sit upon a whirlwind that can flatten all the trees
I shall ride a bucking bronco, way out in the west
And fight a fearsome dragon, clad only in my vest.

When I'm a grown man, I will be a soldier brave
Capture all the terrorists who skulk inside their cave
I'll save the fair young maidens from dragon's claw and flame
And strike that fearsome dragon down, until it is tame.

When I am a grown man, I shall flirt and love the girls
Marry blue-eyes-what's-her-name, with all those crazy curls
I'll buy a great big mansion, with swimming pool out back
Painted on the bottom, a shark all coloured black.

When I am a grown man, I shall still give Mom a kiss
That's the only awesome thing I would really mostly miss
She reads me lovely stories when I'm tucked up tight in bed
Gives me such a sloppy kiss, right here upon my head.

When I'm a grown man, then I shall fly a Phantom jet
I shall fly it to the moon, just for a silly bet
With it, I will loop the loop around the yellow moon
But now Mom is saying, I must go to sleep quite soon.

So I say a fond goodnight, I shall meet you in my dreams
There we can plan our coming hopes, and our naughty schemes
Night descends upon the Earth, and so I make my plan
That I shall be the king of all, when I'm a grown man.

Leslie de la Haye

21st July

Wonderful Wonders

How is it done?
I wonder how.
I've tried and tried to see.

No matter what I do or say
It gets away from me.

I think it must be goblins
Or fairies of some sort.
They must be small
And very quick.
They never do get caught.

If I am slow, they get away.
It's worse when I am quick.
I don't know how to get it right,
I haven't found the trick.

One of these days I'll write a note
And leave it all night long.
I'm sure they'll answer
Then I'll know

Who does put the light on in the fridge?

Eileen O'Brien

22nd July

Pencil Case Politics

'I'm the king of the pencil case,'
Said the fountain pen,
Pulling a rather rude face.

'No you're not. It's me. It's me,'
Said the tall, thin pencil.
Blue and HB.

'I don't agree,' said the paper clip.
'I'm the king and she's the queen,'
Pointing to the felt tip.

'None of you at all can call yourselves king.
That's my title,' said the rubber,
In the shape of a ring.

'Excuse me! But there you're all completely wrong.
I'm the ruler here,
Cos I'm twelve inches long!'

Georgina A Lord

23rd July

Guzzle Guts

Guzzle Guts the squirrel
likes his nuts
that's why he's called Guzzle Guts!

He likes to jump from tree to tree
and oft I find he follows me.
He has no time to stop and chat
too busy going there and back.

'I must be quick, I must be quick
for when it snows it will be thick.'
He wipes his nose and licks his paws
then scurries off to get indoors.

Sure enough in wintertime
Guzzle Guts will be just fine.
Warm and snug in his den
he pops his nose out now and then
just to watch the snowdrops fall
then curls up in a ball
surrounded by his beloved nuts.
Sleep well then, Guzzle Guts!

Helen Scott

24th July

The Spot

I've got a spot, a horrid spot
I wish I hadn't got it
When I go to school each day
Everyone can spot it

I don't know where it came from
It suddenly appeared
It's getting bigger every day
Just as I had feared

I wish it wasn't on my face
Then nobody would see
I could keep it covered up
A secret spot for me

But now it's there just big and red
It nearly drives me mad
It feels like it's the biggest spot
That I have ever had

My friends are understanding
They pretend it isn't there
Though one or two are not so kind
And simply laugh and stare

I long for it to disappear
Get back to being me
I hope it's gone tomorrow
I'll have to wait and see

Barbara Hampson

25th July

Dream Time

When I shut my eyes at night
And snuggle down to bed
Mummy and Daddy are there with me
As images in my head

I dream of all I've done that day
All the fun and the time at play
All the toys, the girls and boys
The things I've seen along the way

The sounds I've heard come back to me
I try to make the words
The chatter from the nursery
The singing of the birds

I move my fingers to try to feel
The toys that are in my head
As I reach out I touch my bear
And snuggle back down to bed

Louise Foster

26th July

The Great Escape

I am on a mission, to get upstairs and play,
I'm shut in downstairs with boring toys every single day.
Sometimes we go into the town or play in swinging chairs,
But mostly I look forward to escaping up those stairs.

My sister's room is full of things she hides away from me,
But I will get into her room just you wait and see.
I watch people come and go by pulling on a lever,
Mummy's friend has just gone through, oh how I'd like to be her.

The time has come to try and reach the lever on the door,
Maybe if I'm on tippy-toes it will open like before.
I'm on my toes and stretching towards my golden goal,
But I'm still not big enough, could I stand upon my bowl?

Mummy is not looking, I find the bowl I like
It was in my cupboard and now's the time to strike.
I put one foot on top the bowl and reach it sure enough,
But however will it open? The door is really tough.

I found my foot was slipping, and wobbling side to side,
As I fell I noticed, the door was open wide.
I am sooo excited and proud what I have done,
Just as I'm escaping, I am whisked up by my mum.

No, no, no, I tried so hard, I worked, I planned, I thought,
And in the moment of my glory, I have just been caught.
Mummy tickles me and laughs, 'You've gotten clever boy!'
She lets me in the garden with my favourite bouncy toy.

So my plan has actually worked, I have managed to escape,
I'll get up the stairs another day, of that make no mistake.

Sarah Hooper

27th July

When A Monkey Came To Visit Me

What would you do if a monkey came to call on you?
Would you ask it in for a biscuit and juice?
If the answer's yes, then beware don't let it loose.
A monkey can be a naughty thing.
From the light shades it might swing,
climb up the curtains that's for certain,
Eat all the fruit in your fruit bowl,
Then throw banana peel on the floor.
Your poor dad might slip, and up he'd soar
And land with a bump on the floor.
It might jump up and down on your mum and dad's bed
And throw the duvet out the door,
Then it would take all the biscuits off the plate,
Eat them all and think it was great.
Then run out of the door and be there no more.
Your dad would shout,' Who dropped this banana peel on the floor?'
Your mum would shout, 'And who's thrown the duvet out the door?'
'And eaten all the biscuits,' she would roar.
And you would say, 'Ah well, you see, a monkey came to visit me.'

Jacqueline Ibbitson

28th July

Who Paints The Rainbows In The Sky?

Where do the rainbows' colours hide
When blue skies turn to grey?
Who paints the arc across the sky
Then folds it safe away?

Where do all the colours go?
I hope it isn't far,
For I would like to pack them up
And put them in a jar.

Do Nature's hands portray the joys
Each time a rainbow's seen?
They really make a lovely job
Whenever they are seen.

Who mixes up the tints and hues
And never spills a drop?
I'd love to find out who they are,
But they never seem to stop.

Who paints the rainbows in the skies
With such artistic flair?
A million times I've searched to find -
But they always disappear!

Malcolm Wilson Bucknall

29th July

Magical Mystery Tour

Darryl and Jane take to the sea
In an old Avon dingy way past its guarantee.
Their journey begins in the long river so wide.
The outboard kicks in and oars put aside.
Darryl fumbles around in the bow of the boat,
He looks for the rod and old wooden float.
Upon looking up, tom Sawyer's sitting there,
Who retorts, *'Come on Huck,'* while fixing a stare.
The outboard is replaced by one long oar,
And so begins the magical mystery tour.
This is now the Mississippi with Tom and Huck
Seeking adventure by hook or by crook.
Big steamers with paddles pass to and fro,
Best to watch out which way to go.
A big steamer approaches and threatens their plight,
Both Tom and Huck are shaking with fright.
'Quick Huck,' said Tom, 'grab hold of those reeds,
We'll haul ourselves in till this traffic has eased.'
Tom climbs out and pulls the boat in,
Huck makes a grab and falls into the swim,
Upon looking up, Tom's gone and Jane's sitting there,
He looks around and not a steamer anywhere.
At the end of the day it's good to pretend,
For some of reality is hard to comprehend.

Darryl Benson

 30th July

Clyde

Clyde Caterpillar crept along,
Past the Alsatian guard dog strong.
Into the huge greenhouse he went,
Crawling over new-laid cement.

Onwards to his personal prey,
Tomatoes, placed in pail that day.
Odour became too much for Clyde,
Which he could smell from the outside.

Ripe-red, inviting in noon sun,
Clyde thought, as he dived in - *what fun!*
But he did not spot lurking bird,
Or showed no sign that he had heard.

Too late! On bucket black bird swooped
And into its beak, Clyde it scooped.
Poor Clyde, only after a treat,
The prize, bird decided to eat.

S Mullinger

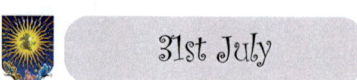 31st July

Freedom To My Budgie

I let my budgie out from its cage
it was my mum who flew into a rage
yelled at me to act my age
so
I've come up to my room
to write down on this page
how do I act nine?
When I'm ten
I'll know then
but now at nine
larking is fine
freedom to my budgie!

Allen Beit

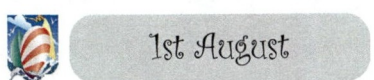

1st August

Magical Dreams

Magical dreams are what we have
When we are very small,
If you try your very best
You can always remember them all.

Fairy castles and palaces
And princesses by the score,
Friendly dragons and animals
Who come knocking at your door.

You want to be a fireman
And be the hero of the day,
Or maybe a train driver
And help people on their way.

Summer holidays with your best friends
Playing all day in the sun,
Hide-and-seek and water games,
Each day is fun, fun, fun.

Whatever it is we wish for
Imagination can make it come true,
Close your eyes, relax and dream
That's all you have to do.

Oh how a dream can make you see
Just how special sleep can be,
So settle down and close your eyes
The magic will start, you'll see.

Tracey Baxter

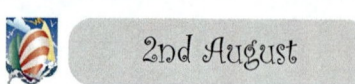

2nd August

Have You Ever?

Have you ever seen a bee without its bumble?
Have you ever seen a turtle take a tumble?
Have you ever seen a flea try to get down on one knee
And get back up again without a grumble?

Have you ever heard a word a squirrel's said?
Have you ever seen a centipede in bed?
Have you ever seen a whale try to stand up on its tail?
Have you ever seen a bat made out of bread?

Have you ever seen a python lose its wriggle?
Have you ever seen a blackbird give a giggle?
Have you ever seen a carrot the same colour as a parrot,
Or a cow who likes to sing and dance and jiggle?

Have you ever seen a bee without its bumble?
Have you ever seen a tree lie down and mumble?
All these things might not be true so I'll leave it up to you,
But while you're out be careful you don't stumble.

Nik Perring

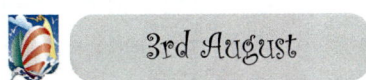 3rd August

The Talking Cat?

A man walked past a cat sitting on a fence,
The cat said, 'Excuse me, could I borrow fifty pence?'
The man looked at him in amazement as the cat smiled at him,
Could this be true, how could it be?
'I'm going to the park and would like an ice cream.'
No, it can't be real, it must be a dream.
Reaching into his pocket he searched around,
Plenty of twenty pences but not one fifty to be found.
He apologised to the cat and went on his way.
Had that just happened? He really couldn't say.
The next day the cat was there again,
He crossed over the road to see his feline friend.
'Hello, how are you today?' the man asked the cat.
The cat just looked at him from where he sat.
No answer, so he asked him one more time.
People were starting to look at the man, like he was out of his mind.
The cat sat up and yawned as he turned his head,
Walking away, 'Miaow!' was all he said.
'No wait, I've got that fifty pence!'
The cat just kept on walking, it didn't make sense.
Had it really just all been a dream?
That's certainly how it was beginning to seem.
The man walked away looking more confused than ever.
The cat turned and said, 'Really, I thought these humans were supposed to be clever!'

Zoë Thompson

4th August

House Of Roses

There is a house of roses
Deep in the sunflower wood
Where sunbeams live and play
As little sunbeams should.

Sometimes sunbeams leave the wood
And return when it's dark outside.
It's never dark in the sunflower wood,
There's no dark place to hide.

The house of roses always shines
In the sunflower wood of light
And all the sunbeams live there
When the world is full of night.

George Coombs

 5th August

Untitled

Matthew, Mark, Mitch and Mike
Teach me how to ride a bike
Then when that's a piece of cake
Teach me how to roller skate
Skate on a board, skate on the ice
Wouldn't that be paradise
Then when that is easy pease
Put me on a pair of water skis
Ski on a board, ski with a kite
Snow ski down a mountainside
Then when I can count to five
Teach me how to paraglide
Over the mountains, over the sea
Out past the reefs where the sharks will be
Just in case I should fall in
Teach me not to sink but swim
Swim like a fish under the sea
Faster than the sharks so they can't catch me
Then if I am still alive
Teach me how to do skydive
Surf on a board, surf on the net
Fly me to the moon by Easy Jet
Bungee jump like a kangaroo
Teach me how to run to Timbuktu
Then when I think I know it all
Teach me how to throw a ball
Throw, catch, kick, score
Shooting goals for evermore
Beam me up to seventh heaven
Make me a football star like Beckham!

Avril Jessey

6th August

Top Banana

If you would enjoy a healthy mañana
Partake each day of a free-range banana.
This delicacy in his jumpsuit of yellow
Is a fiddle-fit frolicsome feast of a fellow.
Up before dawn he is out of his tree
And off through the forest in mad revelry.
Too sharp and too swift to be some primate's lunch
As evening descends he pops back in the bunch.
So pay due respect to that firm, creamy flesh
It's enjoying free-range that makes it so fresh.

Barrie Singleton

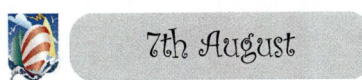

7th August

Sunny

I wish I had a horse.
Not a big one, of course,
Just big enough to sit on and ride,
To go for a trot in the countryside,
Pop in and show to my friends with pride.
Perhaps a little pony.
Hmmm . . .

I'd have to wear a hat
And my boots and all that,
But I'd groom him carefully every day,
Do all those chores with the straw and hay,
Feed him and tend him in every way,
And I think I'd call him - Sunny.
Yes - Sunny!

But ponies cost so much -
And a stable and such -
Dad smiled when I asked him about my idea,
And said, 'You'll just have to wait, I fear.
I really don't think I can see my way clear . . .'
Well, I will have Sunny -
Someday.

Bill Eden

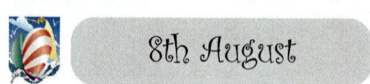

8th August

The Land Down Under

You'll never lose a boomerang,
by throwing it away.
For it would fly right back to you,
as if to say g'day.

It's used by Aborigines,
when they go hunting food.
They also have cave-painted art,
both colourful and crude.

The Great Outback is far away,
from Europe or the States.
And Auzzie citizens do call,
their friends and neighbours 'mates'.

They also have some crazy vets,
who fix up sharks and crocs.
These beasts aren't pets but wild and free,
and cunning as a fox.

And finally, let's not forget,
their furry critters too.
It's where koala bears call home,
as do the kangaroo.

Dickon Springate

9th August

Squirrel Nutkin

Little Squirrel Nutkin
Climbed down from a tree
Ran across the grass
And came right up to me
He had seen me eating
I expect he wanted a share
For he came and joined me
By jumping on a chair.
I fed him from my lunch box
And he quickly nibbled away
Then I gave him some nuts
I'd brought for him that day.
When he had finished eating
He washed his little face
Jumped down from the chair
And ran off at a pace.
The last that I saw of him
Was as he climbed a tree
And when he had reached the top
He turned and looked towards me.

Diana Daley

10th August

LazyTown

In LazyTown in TVLand they're always on the go.
The colours there are mighty grand, a vibrant rich rainbow.
The superhero's really fit - he leaps across the screen.
The villain mucks things up a bit - he gets kicks being mean!
The dainty damsel in distress is perfect for the part.
She always shares her happiness and sings with joyful heart.
She likes to dance from left to right and also up and down.
Without her smiles so pearly white some folks would wear a frown!
Her friends are noble just like her - and what a team they make.
Whatever mishaps may occur, it's action that they take.
The villain will not win the day - although he tries his best.
While Robbie Rotten shouts, 'Hooray!', his schemes will be suppressed!
The hero's airship floats above, amid the clouds so high
Until the damsel calls with love to solve things gone awry.
In LazyTown in TVLand the good guys always win -
The villain's always underhand but heroes don't give in!
That's why we like to watch what's new and how they're getting on
And why we're always feeling blue the moment that they're gone.
So hurry back! Your show's first rate! Vivacious fun to boot!
That Sportacus, he's really great and Stephanie's so cute!

Denis Martindale

11th August

Ten Naughty Children

Ten naughty children standing in a line
One got sick, then there were nine.

Nine naughty children running through a gate
One fell down, then there were eight.

Eight naughty children on their way to Devon
One fell asleep, then there were seven.

Seven naughty children got up to many tricks
One got caught by the headmaster, then there were six.

Six naughty children looking at a hive,
One got stung, then there were five.

Five naughty children thought they saw some straw
One went off, then there were four.

Four naughty children tried to climb a tree
One broke a leg, then there were three.

Three naughty children didn't know what to do
One got bored, then there were two.

Two naughty children tried to eat a bun
One found it rock hard, then there was one.

One naughty child having lots of fun
She went on holiday, then there were none!

Tanzia Haq

12th August

Twinkle

Twinkle, twinkle aeroplane
how I wonder that you stay up there,
up so high and still in view
flying where the sky is blue,
twinkle, twinkle aeroplane
you're the modern Jonah whale.

Twinkle, twinkle aeroplane
night reveals your coloured flares,
lovely colours, green and red
eyes that are white and on your tail,
twinkle, twinkle aeroplane
from your logo I know from where.

Twinkle, twinkle aeroplane
where are you heading high up there,
travelling beneath the sky so blue
magic bird that runs on fuel,
twinkle, twinkle aeroplane
in your belly we go on holidays.

Twinkle, twinkle aeroplane
now so common I don't stare,
yet I envy all in you
travelling on to somewhere new,
twinkle, twinkle aeroplane
dreams fulfilled because of you.

Philip Anthony McDonnell

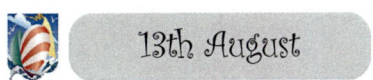

13th August

You'll Never Walk Alone

Mr and Mrs Robin built a cosy little nest
Made of moss and feathers and somebody's old vest.
They hoped to have two chicks or more - or even more than that!
So Robbie Robin dug for worms to keep his Rosie fat.

Rosie sat upon her eggs for three whole weeks,
Till one fine day, she heard some funny beaky squeaks.
Daddy Robin heard them too and fainted with excitement.
He woke to find four tiny heads, and fainted again with delightment!

A few weeks later, Daddy said, 'Those chicks have bright red breasts.
Just listen to them giggling, Mum, and being pesky pests!'
He tried to frown and look so cross and said, 'What's all the hooey?'
Belinda said, 'It's Hughie, Daddy - see, he's gone all bluey.'

Mummy cried, 'Oh my, just look at our poor little Hughie.
My other babes are rosy-red, but Hughie's brightest bluey!'
Mummy held her Hughie tight and cuddled him so near,
'Don't worry, don't, my little chick, you're very, very dear.'

In time the Robin family went off to watch their team,
Hughie wore a bright red shirt, his bright black eyes a-gleam.
And when the great crowd sang their very favourite hymn,
Hughie knew for sure, they were singing it for him.

O Monica Fisher

14th August

No Room For Answers

How does the butter fly?
Where did the flamin go?
Who did the spider spy on?
Does anybody know?

Who did the robin rob?
What did the adder add?
Where did the ante lope to?
Are cheetahs really bad?

Does the cricket play for England?
And how does he hold his bat?
Why does the grizzly bear grizzle?
And why is a gnat not fat?

Do jellyfish go to parties?
Do angelfish say their prayers?
Would a dragonfly breathe fire
If you caught him unawares?

Who did the croco dial?
What did the chimpan see?
What is the cuckoo cooking?
Could I go round for tea?

My head is packed with questions.
It's full up to the brim.
How will I find the room
To fit the answers in?

Sarah Fuller

15th August

A Cautionary Tale Of A Little Boy Who Would Eat Anything

Christopher was a little boy who
Was very fond of eating glue.
His mum said, 'Do not eat that muck.
You'll find your stomach will get stuck.'
He ate the plate, the knife, the fork,
His mouth so full he could not talk.
His mother soon despaired of him.
'It's a very dangerous whim
To eat all the junk that you can find.'
Warned his mother, 'And to speak my mind
If you continue, you will die.'
'No, I won't. That's a lie!'
Out of the fire he ate the coal
And in the garden he caught a mole
Where he consumed the poor thing raw,
Its fur, its whiskers and its paw.
He ate up half a dining chair
And his baby sister's hair.
He ate the furniture made of wood
And his little sister's hood.
(Bought because she had no hair.
Her brother had eaten it for a dare.)
He ate the poison for the mice
And as he died he said, 'That's nice!'

Fleur Pyves

16th August

The Bumblecockalorum

The Bumblecockalorum in Bongoland at their zoo,
Wakes up everyone each morning
With his *buzzadoodledoo*.
He makes a really dreadful noise
But people all have said,
He's better than alarm clocks
To get you out of bed.
He struts around the zoo all day
With his adoring hens,
The keepers know it's better
Than to shut them up in pens.
He's funny and he's furry and he's frightening to see
'Cause the back of him is like a cock,
The front of him a bee.
There's not another one like him,
And if you searched around,
There's no place in the universe
Another will be found.
And if you read your history books
Stone Age to Roman Forum,
You'd never find they'd one like him,
The Bumblecockalorum.

Margaret B Baguley

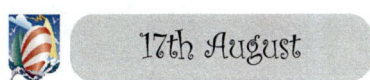 17th August

My Crazy Pup

Oh Jupiter, oh Jupiter,
I think you're getting stupider.
I told you not to suck my scarf
But all you do is choke and laugh -

And now you're twisted in a knot
And wrapped around a flower pot
And if you tug much more, my pup,
You'll squeeze my neck and I'll sick up!

Rosemary Keith

18th August

Humpty Dumpty

Humpty Dumpty
Sat on a plate,
Feeling so warm
He could hardly wait.
Suddenly
Down came a fork,
Humpty Dumpty
Felt like a dork.

Humpty Dumpty
Sat in a cup,
Feeling so tight,
He couldn't sit up.
Suddenly
Down came a spoon,
Humpty Dumpty
Started to swoon.

Humpty Dumpty
Sat on the toast,
Feeling so hot
He started to roast.
Suddenly
Down came a knife
Humpty Dumpty
Rolled for his life.

Humpty Dumpty
Lay on the floor,
Cracked and dazed
And feeling so sore.
Suddenly
He started to shake,
His poor little yolk
Was about to break!

Joy Weare

19th August

Roaming Romans

I saw a Roman roaming,
A roaming round in Rome;
A roaming Roman roaming round
On a road in Rome.

The Roman roamed in rows of Romans,
In rows of Romans roaming;
Rows of roaming Romans roaming
On a road in Rome.

An aroma roaming round in Rome,
Roamed along the Roman road,
Roamed along the Roman road,
Where rows of Romans roamed.

The aroma roamed through roaming Romans,
Aroming Romans as they roamed;
Aroming roaming rows of Romans,
Roaming on a road in Rome.

(Which is how they had Roman scent-urians.)

Kevin Baskin

20th August

Mice Beware!

A mouse and a crocodile sprawled out on a bank
Enjoying the midday sun.
They'd closed their eyes and spread out flat
Well away from everyone.

They lay spread there for an hour or more
Till a cloud it drifted by
Then the slight cool breeze awoke them both
With a great big lazy sigh.

The mouse got up and he stretched his legs
Saying, 'I think I will go for a swim.'
'Sounds good to me,' said the crocodile
With that so he followed him.

They splashed around in the murky depths
Till both were tuckered out.
So - they made for the shore to catch their breath
Then had a gentle walk about.

'I'm hungry now!' the mouse he said
As he sniffed into the breeze.
'What I wouldn't do just right now
For a hunk of some Cheddar cheese.'

'Well you know,' said croc, 'now that you mention it
I haven't eaten for a day or two,
But there's nothing here for me to eat
So, what do you think we should do?'

Mouse looked at the croc and he felt so sad
As he wondered what he should do.
'I'm much too small to go and hunt
To try and get something to eat for you.'

20th August

Croc turned to the mouse. He smiled and he said
'Why don't you close your eyes
Then if you count to ten I guarantee
You'll have a big surprise.'

Mouse did just that and he began to count
From one to the number ten,
But with one swift swoop from the crocodile -
He was chewed like a midget gem.

Now listen, mice - listen one and all
Especially those whose friend is a crocodile -
Never close your eyes,
Never count to ten
And never trust is hungry smile!

Cora Barras

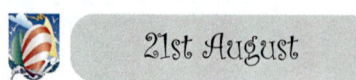

21st August

Locked Out

The Teletubbies got locked out of their house,
Only because they were scared of a little old mouse.
Old MacDonald tried the door using a skeleton key,
But got stung on the thumb by a buzzing bumblebee.
Little Jack Horner even came out of his corner,
While Winnie the Pooh cried, 'Can Piglet help too?'
As Postman Pat tied a rope from the door to his van,
Bob the Builder was shouting, 'Oh yes we can.'
SpongeBob Squarepants declared, 'I'm ready, I'm ready,'
While the line to the van was held amazingly steady.
Rosie and Jim were amazed as they sat on their barge,
How the helping crowd had become exceedingly large.
When the line broke and everyone landed in an almighty heap,
Away in the distance they could hear a *beep, beep*.
Along came Fireman Sam, who got them into their house,
Where there was not even a sign of the little old mouse!

Lyndsay Lynch

 22nd August

Horrible Henry

Horrible Henry's got habits so horrid
He picks at the spots all over his forehead
Girls won't sit next to him
They go sit elsewhere
He just makes rude faces
Pretends not to care

Horrible Henry is called lots of names
He's always excluded from other kids' games
He trips up the boys and he pinches the girls
God help the ones who have heads full of curls!
Nothing can stop him whilst he has no friend
He's driving his teachers right round the bend

Anne Elibol

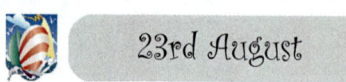

23rd August

Ella's Secret

One night when Ella could not sleep
She got up from her bed and dressed
Then went outside into the garden deep
Surprised she did not feel oppressed.

Going amongst some grasses, growing untidily
She felt a presence close beside her,
'Who is there?' she asked quite politely.
Feeling pleased when a voice said, 'I'm Kerr.'

'What a peculiar name, please show yourself to me.'
Suddenly beside her was a yellow gnome with a pointed head.
'Why, you are a funny colour, that I can see.'
'Why, don't you like it?' and made himself turn red.

'Oh yes, dear friendly Kerr, I love all colours.
Have you lived in my garden forever?'
'Yes,' he replied, 'this is my family home.'
'Lovely, you must all be so jolly clever.'

'Then do come and see us in our homes.'
So Ella went with Kerr and laughing with delight,
'Why, you are so pretty, I will call you my rainbow gnomes,'
Ella enjoyed meeting them often, and thought, *I feel no fright*.

After this she visited Kerr's home, talking to them all.
The families all lived together so merrily.
So she kept the secret of her new-found friends,
An lovely event, which she enjoyed so happily.

Marjorie Busby

 24th August

Who Am I?

Children like me very much, I make a lovely pet as such,
I like to be stroked a lot, let's find out what I've got.
Pointed ears, lovely green eyes, food I like to eat is mice,
Quite long whiskers, bushy tail, fur coat's lines are dark and pale.
I don't like water, dogs or vets,
So who am I, kids? Guessed yet?

I could be big, I could be small,
I could be short, I could be tall.
My ears could be drooped or pointed right up,
My tail could be bushy or small like a rosebud.
Sometimes I must be trained or exercised a lot,
I make a 'man's best friend' - that's what I've always thought.
I don't like cats, I don't like vets,
So who am I, kids? Guessed yet?

Anna Bayless

25th August

Puffle Puff

There was once a Puffle Puff as proud as can be
Who took me to a land far across the sea
Night and day we were afloat
Happy as can be on the Puffle Puff's boat

When we arrived what an amazing place
Lots of Puffle Puffs with a smile on their face
All came running to shake my hand
Then someone shouted, 'Let's strike up the band.'

Magical music did fill the air
All my troubles went, I did not have a care
Dancing along a blue winding street
To the Puffle Puff's house where I was offered a seat

A big table was brought and a feast we had
But then the Puffle Puff did look sad
I asked, 'What's the matter, what is wrong?'
'Can you help us,' it said, 'can you teach us a song?'

So I started to hum a simple tune
And burst into song for all in the room
All the Puffle Puffs listened as I sang
When all of a sudden there was a big bang

I jumped off my seat and bumped my head
Then I awoke to find I was on my bed
To the land of the Puffle Puff I had been
You can go there too but you need to dream

Do you want to go to Puffle Puff land?
To hear the music of the Puffle Puff band?
If this is your wish, this is what you must do
Close your eyes, go to sleep, it's all up to you

Mike Tracey

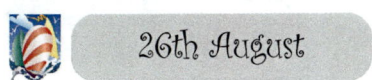 26th August

My Friend The Cuckoo

A great big bird flew past me
it looked like a cuckoo upside down
he was wearing wellies on his wings
and had a face just like a clown

I asked if he would stay and play with me a while
he only said, 'Cuckoo, cuckoo,'
which made me laugh and smile

He landed on the washing line
where all our clothes hung out
and then he did a naughty thing and Mum began to shout

She rushed inside and got her brush and chased him into the sky
he flew off with such a rush
he didn't even say goodbye

Jessie Bruce

27th August

Melissa's Brother

Melissa had a brand new brother,
They called him baby Lee,
Oh good, she thought, he'll be such fun,
He'll dance and jump and sing and run
And chase the rainbows in the sun
And come and play with me.

At length (after forever), he grew big enough to 'be'.
The time arrived, excitement high,
Mummy was away three nights, Melissa had such awful fights
With older brother Sky.
She wasn't going to let them know how much she missed her mother so,
After all she had her pride, she wasn't even three!

But when this brand new bundle home from hospital came,
Instead of being friendly, it refused to say her name.
The little beast, the little brat, it looked more like a wrinkled rat.
It screamed, it yelled, was sick and poo'd,
Was full of wind and wee,
'I wish they'd take him in the car and dump him in the sea'.

Mum's friends said, 'Coo, he's lovely, aren't you a *lucky* girl?
You must be good, you must behave. No fuss, no noise, give back his toys.
He needs to sleep. You're grown up now. Stop hitting baby Lee.'
She worked so hard to teach him. To show him who was boss,
But when she tried to pinch him, Mummy got *very* cross.

And then, one day (with no one looking),
She came to his side,
Inside her little heart swelled with sisterly pride.
She smiled at him a sister's love and baby Lee smiled too,
He laughed, he gurgled, kicked his feet
And chortled loud with glee.
The bond of love transfixed in time, cemented in the physical realm,
Ensured from that day on, best friends they'd always be.

Jennifer Densham

28th August

God Is Fair

If you happened to be born as a bug,
Or worse, a really miserable slug,
Don't get angry, don't curse and swear,
There's always someone out there,
That could very well make you feel real smug.

Heard about the doctor who's scared of blood
Or the earthworm who's terrified of mud?
The school teacher who's scared of children?
The lion who's afraid of a kitten?
What about the pig who loves hamburgers?
The turkey who looks forward to Christmas?
The nun who keeps thinking she's a monk?
The pussycat who's actually a skunk!

Everyone has a story to tell,
Everyone thinks they're living in Hell,
But God is fair,
Do not despair,
Things may not be half as bad as they smell.

Or would you rather be born a dodo?
Worse, an awful bloodsucking mosquito?
A clam who is terrified of drowning,
A pilot who has a fear of flying
And would you prefer to be a lobster
Or become a boring old cucumber?
A jellyfish who thinks he's a shark,
A ghost who is terrified of the dark!

So you see, it cannot be all that bad,
Life has to go on, don't feel so sad,
Try to pull yourself together,
Nobody will live forever,
Sometimes it helps if we're all a little mad.

Ken Lou

29th August

There's A Monster Under My Bed

My room is dark and scary
I see shadows that look like scary monsters coming after me
The floorboards creak
I hear mice squeak
I don't like going to bed even though I have my ted
Mum tucks me up in tight
And I tell her to leave on the landing light
Then I try to go to sleep but I am sure I am not alone
I see a shadow crawl under my bunk bed
It looks like a big lion's head
I peep out of my covers hoping it won't see me
I shout, 'Mum, Mum, Muuuuum'
But she ignores me because she thinks I am having a dream
Oh I think that is mean.
The monster under my bed now makes a funny sound
Like a soft roaring noise, I think it is the black hound
I am scared; it sounds like it is getting near
Argh! it has jumped on top of me I fear
It rubs against my face, it is furry
Oh no, it is going to eat me
Then the monster lets out a miaow
I lift my head up; phew it is only my cat, Moppet
From now on I won't be afraid of going to bed.

Sasha Lyon

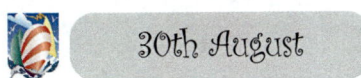 30th August

Bedtime Blues

It's time for my bed now
And I'm feeling blue
I don't want to go
As there's so much to do

I might paint the carpet
With toothpaste galore
Or cover with hairspray
The living room door

I could drop the toilet roll
Into the lav
I may even hide
The remote from my dad

Put parts of my ant farm
In big sister's bed
Dismember her teddy
That'd make her see red

To get at my mum
I would hide all her keys
And not give them back
'Til she said pretty please

In actual fact, and in all modesty
There are millions of things
Which could entertain me
Proving devilishly aggravating

However, my mother
She will not see sense
Insisting it's bedtime
With no arguments!

Sharon Spencer

31st August

Little Jack

Little Jack sits in a classroom
With tears in his eyes.
He'd like to leave the room soon,
But he still sits there and cries.

'What happened?' the janitor asks,
'You know, boys shouldn't cry.
Your teachers gave too many tasks
Or the lessons were too dry?'

Little Jack still sobs and sighs,
He fears to raise his little head.
'My friends and teachers were nice
Oh, I feel so stupid and ashamed.

My geography teacher told me today
To find the Suez Canal on the map,
But the canal had oddly gone astray
Please, look at the atlas on my lap.'

The janitor sets about leafing through
This colourful, thick, interesting book.
'It's difficult to catch on - it's true,
But we've the Suez Canal here, look!'

Little Jack's eyes cheered up at once.
He was embarrassed but very content
With the sudden discovery - he cries:
'I looked for it on another continent!'

Jolanta Gradowicz

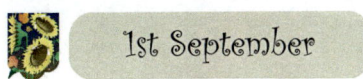 1st September

Harry

First time in the playground
He's as happy as Larry,
'Hello everybody,
My name's Harry.'
Off he goes into school
And sits next to Barry,
'Hello,' he says,
'My name's Harry.'
The teacher looks across the room
And says her name's Miss Clarry,
So of course up he jumps
And says, 'My name's Harry.'
As everyone goes to assembly
In the hall with Mr Farry,
He looks down at this smiling face
Who shouts out, 'My name's Harry.'
He has his classes through the day
And his lunch with a girl called Carry,
He offers her his apple
And tells her, 'My name's Harry.'
It's home time at last
As he gets the bus to Darry,
Everyone in the playground shouts,
'Goodbye, my name's Harry.'

Stephanie Teasdale

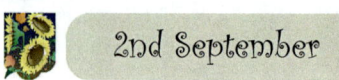 2nd September

The Weather

I didn't do my homework, Miss,
The flood swallowed it up, Miss.
I couldn't write about my car, Miss,
The hail made it ill, Miss.
I couldn't go to sleep, Miss,
The earthquake shook my house, Miss.
I couldn't go sailing, Miss,
The winds wrecked my boat, Miss.
I couldn't go to hospital, Miss,
The building got snowed down, Miss.
I can't go swimming, Miss,
The water is frozen, Miss.
I can't do games, Miss,
The sunshine gives me a stroke, Miss.
I can't wear my hat, Miss,
The wind blows it away, Miss.
I can't play the match, Miss,
The snow made it unsafe, Miss.
I can't come to school, Miss,
The lightning burned it down, Miss.

Samyukta Aryasomayahjula

3rd September

Flying

(Inspired by the story 'Peter Pan and Wendy' written by J M Barrie. He donated all rights to the story to Great Ormond Street Hospital whose charity still benefits from the royalties)

'Can I really fly like Peter Pan?'
'No, my boy, no one on Earth can fly.
But if your heart is light with love and joy,
Then, in dreams you can reach the sky.
Dreams can take you past the second star,
To that magic land where children fly,
Where mermaids sing and fairies flit about,
You can find it all, in your mind's eye.

Imagination is the special key,
Use it well to open your mind's doors,
You will fly just like that magic boy
And find that the universe is yours.
When, in grown-up years, you must live here,
In this world with all its work and care,
Always keep the child inside alive
And you will find that you can go back there.
Find a quiet spot, relax and dream,
Call upon that child from years ago.
Let him lead you back to Never-Land
And show you the way to fly, once more.

Pamela Evans

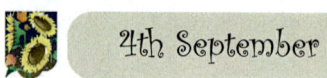 4th September

Scarecrow

In open field behind the farm,
Away from sight and sound and harm,
A scarecrow stands in sea of corn
In jacket patched and sleeves all torn.
He meets the night and greets the dawn,
He has no movement, speaks no words,
But standing there, he scares the birds.
In trousers frayed, tied up with string,
He braves the winter, welcomes spring.
A turnip head and carrot nose
And hair of straw that never grows,
He stands in silence,
Feet and toes in tattered socks and boots undone,
He drips in rain and dries in sun.

His peace was shattered one sad day
When farmer, tired of bailing hay,
Made haste to plough the furrowed ground
Churning everything around, made
A dreadful grating, whirring sound.
The scarecrow's back was snapped in two
And then his mangled coat and shoe
Fast round the blade, were sliced straight through!
The carrot, straw and turnip head
Were chewed and pulped and crudely spread.

A pile of sawdust, bits of rags,
The scarecrow's 'life' just stuffed in bags.
Though farmer looked he never saw
That shredded by his giant claw
The faithful scarecrow was no more.

Lesley Elaine Greenwood

 5th September

My Friend

I have a friend, his name is Tim
His terribly tall and he's terribly thin
When the wind comes whistling by
It takes poor Tim right into the sky
So I tie some string around his toes
Then I can follow him wherever he goes

Glenda Doller

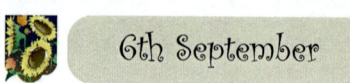 **6th September**

Asleep With Nana

Sleep with windows open to the night
and keep the child within awake
to hear the rapping at the window
when the spirits come to call.
Hold tight the duvet when the dog growls
because it may be the pirates come
or Peter, with his Tinkerbell
flying from the *Never-Never-Land*
where the Lost Boys still wait
for a mother's love to grip them tight.

Little boys do not grow up
they only leave behind their youth
to stumble over in the night
when dreaming speaks a truth.

Stephen Page

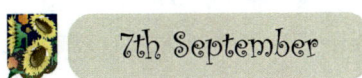 7th September

Grandpa

This poem is for Grandpa, the old man with no hair,
You really cannot miss him as he snores within his chair.
With slippers on and eyes shut tight and hands clasped on full belly,
He relaxes after Sunday lunch whilst we all watch the telly.

The snoring starts to worsen, every week is just the same,
The rumbling and the rasping sounds just like a diesel train.
It's like being on a station, and there's nothing we can do,
We stand behind the yellow line as Grandpa rushes through.

The room shakes like an earthquake, where buildings swing and sway,
And bits of concrete hit the ground as Grandpa snores away.
But when I look at Grandpa, who wears an old string vest,
I know I love him very much, my grandpa is the best.

Pete Hazell

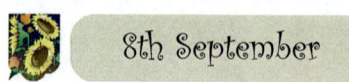

8th September

Give Your Nan A Kiss

Give your nan a kiss
No way, she smells of wee
I'm telling you right now
She's not kissing me!

Do you want a smack?
Now why would I want that?
I'd rather have some chocolate
Or a brand new riding hat.

Don't you be so cheeky
Go straight up to your room!
Great, now I'll have a better view
When you fly off on your broom.

Right, that's it, you're grounded
What a big relief
Now at least I'm free to go
And pick my nose in peace.

Louise Smith

9th September

Peaceful Coexistence

Said the glamorous poppy to the wheat,
'I do wish the sun would shine more,
It's a pity you're not even pretty,
Oh dear, life is such a bore.'

Said the wheat,
'You seem to have joined the wrong set
And if you don't like us, push off,
You're simply a silly coquette,
Flapping your petals to show off
And catch the attention of the wind,
In the end, he'll totally deflower you,
Or perhaps a mad poet will come and devour you.
Of beauty, of course, I've no need
And many a poor mouth I'll feed,
I assure you there's no nonsense in my full head.'

Said the poppy,
'Oh please don't be so wise and mighty,
Forgive me for what I've said,
Perhaps I am a bit flighty,
Dear wheat, you've got such a nice head
And I'm sure you'll make very good bread.'

When one has to live in the same field,
It's wise to keep one's mind veiled.

Mary Frances Mooney

10th September

A Child's Verse

(For the NSPCC)

For all you children everywhere,
here's a verse to show I care.
Fight and win for you I do,
vanquish pain, forever true.
World out there for you to win,
conquer hurt, nay, everything.
Would I wish upon a star,
be Superman, go fast and far.
Drive evil out to extinction,
all nastiness we do shun.
In every form or shape or way,
I'll win the war for peace to stay.
Tranquil nights and peaceful days,
what a thing to sing in praise.
Hate's bereft from serene gaze,
heart's at rest in softest haze.
Love has won, charity raise
its curtain now, to my amaze.
Girls and boys I fight to save.

C Thornton

 11th September

Our Tiger

There's a tiger in our garden
We're not sure how or why
It gave a roar to the girl next door
And made her baby cry

I saved him half my peas and chips
Then sneaked out of the door
The tiger ate the entire plate
Then gave another roar

Dad said we can't keep him
I pleaded that he stay
Mum said no, he's got to go
The zoo took him away

Now I go to visit him
As often as I please
On Saturday, when the keeper's away
I feed him chips and peas

Sharon Adkins

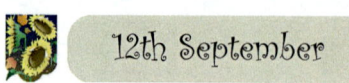 12th September

Untitled

When I grow up I want to be a doctor or a nurse.
I'll carry stethoscopes, vaccines and cleansers in my purse.
But then I think about it: can I be brave and strong?
The sight of needles makes my feet go numb for so long.

When I grow up I want to be a teacher at the school.
I will teach kids to read and write, and follow any rule.
But then I think about it: is teaching made for me?
It seems my teachers always have more homework than me.

When I grow up I want to have a special kind of job.
I'll travel often and will make new friends around the globe.
But then I think about it: can I leave Mom and Dad
For so long, be on my own? It makes me very sad.

What shall I be when I grow up? I have to have a plan!
I guess I'll be whatever I decide, want and can.

Julia Gallego

 13th September

Fairy Lake

Over the moon
Beyond the mists
Lies Fairy Lake
Where Queen Lilith sits upon her throne
On an island in the middle of Fairy Lake
Making sure order stays in motion
And peace reigns.

Fairies glide over the lake
Dropping dust from their wings
Re-energising the mystic water
That brings forth new life
From one dimension to another.

For no other body of water can be like this lake
Slow moving
All nurturing
Full of life
The bluest of blues
And the greenest of greens.

Free of pollution and death
Harmony among all that resides in it.

No cloudy skies
Or dark nights
Only a constant warm day.

For it is from Fairy Lake
That all life originated from
The bluest of blues
And the greenest of greens
My ancient Fairy Lake.

Andrew J Ball

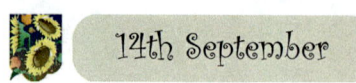
14th September

I've Got A Good Excuse, Miss

My paper flew out the window, Miss
It's landed in a puddle,
It's all wet and the ink's run, Miss
And the writing is in a muddle.

The dog has eaten my homework, Miss
We took him to the vet,
My maths gave him a bellyache, Miss
He's terribly upset.

I can't eat my school dinner, Miss
This custard is way too cold,
It's very lumpy too, Miss
It must be *very* old.

I haven't got my PE kit, Miss
It shrunk in the tumble drier,
I'm not telling you fibs, Miss
I'm not a little liar!

Sorry I'm late for school, Miss
But our car wouldn't start,
We had to take it to the garage, Miss
And buy it a new part.

I wasn't naughty in the playground, Miss
I didn't throw my wrapper on the ground,
The wind blew it out of my hand, Miss
But I chased it round and round.

I'm telling you the truth, Miss
Everything I've said is true,
You don't look like you believe me, Miss
Oh now what shall I do?

Stevie Gregg (8)

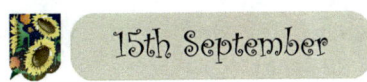 15th September

At The Bottom Of The Garden

There is a little man,
Whose name is Dan,
He lives in a plant pot in the garden.

He has a red nose,
And long, long toes,
He works all day in the garden.

His clothes are green
And cannot be seen,
As he hides away in the trees,
At the bottom of the garden.

He comes out at night,
When the stars are bright,
Where he plays with the fieldmice,
At the bottom of the garden.

No one would guess
That amongst the flower beds
That a little man lives
At the bottom of the garden.

Eileen W O'Brien

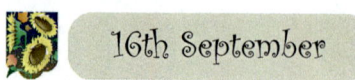

16th September

Rancid Raymond

Little Rancid Raymond's mother, called him in to have his supper
He really thought she shouldn't see the dead mouse or the bumblebee
So in his rucksack, they did go, she wouldn't find them there and so,
He thought maybe just one thing more, before he reached the kitchen door
Rancid Raymond's smile grew wide as on the ground he now espied
Quite disgusting and cut in three, the longest worm you did ever see
Bending down he picked it up and put it in his drinking cup
Sitting at the table he, began to get quite fidgety when Mother poured a cup of tea
Then handed it to Rancid's pa, who drank it down, all's well so far
But when Pa's mouth did open wide, three ugly worms crawled from inside,
Mother fainted and Dad was sick, Rancid must think of something quick,
Bending down to help his mother, Rancid very soon discovered
His rucksack toppled over and, it certainly wasn't filled with sand
Papa's sick was on the floor, all over Mother what is more
And there beside her for all to see, one dead mouse and a bumblebee!
Putting the dead mouse in the bin, he quickly wiped his father's chin,
He'd have to write a 'sorry' letter, but Papa now looked so much better
Mother didn't look too well, when she was poorly he could tell,
He cleaned her up but he could see, that wriggling, buzzing, bumblebee
Covered in sick from Papa's tea, this his mother must not see,
Gradually she came around, and lifted her head from the ground,
'Whatever happened?' she did ask, and now for Rancid's final task
And as he leaned to pull her free, he put his foot on the bumblebee,
It splattered underneath his shoe, and he mixed it in like new-made glue
Mother, now upon her feet, chastises Pa and he can't compete
With all the shouting going on, Rancid knows he's in the wrong
He watches now the worm re-form and wriggle out across the lawn
And thinks about his papa's vomit, which left his mouth like a space-age rocket
It's stale and stinking on the floor so Rancid creeps out through the door
He's going to see what he can see, under a bush or beneath a tree
And as he goes, he pops his pimples, and feels the pus run down his dimples
Yellow and warm he takes a lick, now what's that beneath that old damp brick?

Jackie Davies

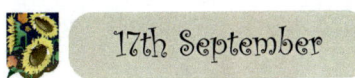 17th September

Autumn's Glory

Red and gold and russet brown,
from the trees the leaves drop down,
scattering their colours on the ground.

Copper and gold they lie before us,
while all around the trees in chorus
mourn for summer's vanished days.

Coloured with a touch of flame,
no two leaves are quite the same,
autumn's glorious dying boast.

They crackle, too, like sticks on fire,
as little children never tire
of throwing, kicking, scattering them.

A sea of dying brown they lie,
yet still with strength left to defy,
grey dead winter's onward march.

Bernard Fyles

18th September

The Attic

Way up in the attic
When night-time has come
All the toys on the shelves
Will have lots of fun
Toy soldiers will march
While the pipers play
And the dolls will dance
The long hours away
Teddy bears will picnic
And tops merrily spin
Bells start to chime
And a nightingale sing
Soft fluffy rabbits
All hop up and down
And there is a big soppy grin
On the face of the clown
There is a cradle that rocks
And a baby doll in it
A bagatelle prize
And you can win it
And you can be sure
Before morning has come
All the toys on the shelves
Will have lots of fun.

Eileen Barlow

19th September

A Flight Of Fancy

The little blue tit preened his feathers; he had to look his best,
It was a lovely sunny day and it was the day he left the nest.
His mummy and his daddy had shown him how to fly,
And today he rose up from the ground to greet the clear blue sky.

His parents felt so proud of him as they watched from a nearby tree.
He remembered all that they had taught. It was what they wished to see.
His little blue tit sister joined him there but couldn't fly so high.
She tried but couldn't manage it, she wouldn't even try.

She flew back home to rest and felt a little sad,
Her parents weren't so proud of her, and that was really bad.
Her brother joined her in the nest: 'Come on, it's so good.'
But she could only wish her wish - 'I don't ever think I could.'

'Come on,' he said. 'Climb on my back. I'll take you for a ride.'
'Oh, I'm far too scared.' And he said, 'You won't know until you've tried.'

He put her gently on his back and their parents watched them fly,
Her father said, 'She's very brave. I thought she'd never try.'
They watched them as they took off together and swooped into the sky so blue.
Their parents looked on excitedly. 'It is really great, shall we try it too?'

Ronald Moore

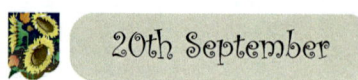 20th September

Twilight Time

The sun is slipping from the sky;
A pale light fills my room.
It's twilight time, so I'm in bed
And will be sleeping soon.

I close my eyes and drift away,
To find those far-off places,
Where magic dwells; and dreams
Are made of happy smiling faces.

Claire Louise Stendall

21st September

The Giant

In the deep forest a tall giant stands.
His arms are his branches, his twigs are his hands.
His trunk is his body, his roots are his feet.
A friendlier giant no one could meet.

He shelters the birds from the sun and the rain,
But this giant has never been heard to complain
When children play near him shrieking in fun,
Around his huge middle they dance and they run.

They shuffle through his leaves which in autumn fall down
In colours of yellow, of orange and brown.
Gaps in his foliage, quick squirrels jump through,
Whilst high there above them the pale ringdoves coo.

Some days you'll hear magpies and maybe a cat
Or a home-making woodpecker's ratatat-tat.
All of them lively and busy as bees
When they swarm on this giant, the king of the trees.

The sheep and the cattle come cropping the grass
Amongst his thick roots as they quietly pass.
Butterflies in summer alight on his bark,
And moths in the evening flit around him when dark.

He stands high and mighty, this oak tree so old.
Through centuries he's lived through heat and the cold.
Deep snows of winter and blustery gales,
As brave as a giant in child's fairy tales.

Laura Föst

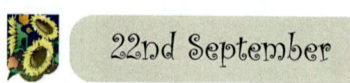

22nd September

A Funny Poem

A man was trying to cross the street,
Many times he tried,
I said, 'There's a zebra crossing down the road,'
'Good luck to him,' he replied.

There was a short-sighted hedgehog,
Always in a rush,
To see his latest girlfriend,
An old scrubbing brush.

Decorated with stripes,
Animals called zebras,
Often being mistaken
For ponies wearing pyjamas.

Standing in the fish shop,
In the queue, a chap looked pale,
He'd seen in the restaurant,
A man-eating whale.

A poor little butterfly,
Not allowed in the local hall,
The reason for the refusal,
Because it was a moth ball.

There was a rabbit with a shiny nose,
To shine, it drove him round the bend,
Because his little powder puff,
Was at the other end.

A frog was very unhappy,
You could say, very sad,
Not only was he miserable,
He was hopping mad!

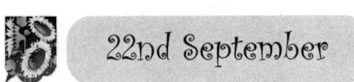

22nd September

My dog thought she saw a fairy,
As it flitted by,
Poor dog had got bad eyesight,
It was a dragonfly.

The new barmaid had a lot to learn,
Although she was very pretty,
She didn't know when the glass was half full,
Or when it was half empty.

An Australian farmer,
Produced something quite unique,
A pretty woollen jumper,
By crossing a kangaroo with a sheep.

This is the funniest poem
I have ever done,
But, if there were no fools,
There would be no fun.

Jeff Northeast

 **23rd September**

Pink

Down by the river there were a few shops,
the village hall right at the end,
then there were houses with neat little lawns,
a church, very small but quite grand.

Right in the corner and tucked in-between
house number six and house number four,
house number five had a window each side
next to a shocking-pink door.

Bert lived there with his very old dog
who always had on a pink coat . . .
just like his master, Timmy looked warm,
good job that pink suited them both!

When it was cold in the house with pink door
Bert sat in his chair made of oak,
his fire was lit, he cared not a bit
that the chimney was churning pink smoke.

Inside the neat house, it was all very pink -
a pink carpet, pink curtains as well,
in parlour and kitchen, upstairs too I guess
Bert loved pink - 'twas easy to tell!

Down by the river they all loved old Bert,
his kindness was known all around,
shocking-pink roses he grew just to give
to lonely folk who were housebound.

When Bert died one day, he was aged eighty-five,
he looked at that river from high,
the people all knew Bert was having a laugh
when they saw the shocking-pink sky!

Connie Anderson

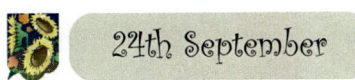 24th September

The Butterflew

Today I saw a butterfly
that fluttered round and round the sky.
I went right in and told my mum
and she said, 'My and oh and um!'

She said, 'I can't believe my eyes.
I never knew that butter flies
I didn't know that butter flew.
I really have to phone the zoo.'

She phoned the zoo and they said, 'Ooo!
We didn't know that butter flew.
We didn't know that butter flies
and melts and drips down through the skies.

We wonder would you bring us some
that we may see and ho and hum?'
'Of course,' said Mum, 'we'll be right there.
We'll even try to bring a pair.

My darling boy will be quite famed,
for flying butter he has tamed.'
'Oh Mum,' said I, 'such a to-do!
Why did you have to phone the zoo?

I didn't say that butter flies
and melts and drips down through the skies.
Why did you say to me 'Oh my,
I really can't believe my eyes'?
You never saw that butter flies
and melts and drips from way up high.
I said I saw a butterfly
that fluttered round and round the sky.'

Helen McKinlay (New Zealand author)

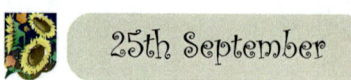

25th September

A Bedtime Story

There once lived a beautiful bird
High in a tree in a forest
In a nest she built with no dirt
So proud, minded her own business

Under the same tree lived a mole
Dug a tunnel through the darkness
His humble home was just a hole
Saw the dark side of the forest

Said the mole, 'Please, Bird, let me be
In your beautiful nest so new
High, very high in the huge tree
I just want to see the forest view'

'No,' said Bird, 'not ever
Will I let you in my home, Mole,
I ask to see your home? Never
Was that my desire, my goal'

Then one night furious thunder
Hit the forest and then lightning
Bird's nest, feathers blew asunder
As the stormy wind reigned as king

She landed in front of Mole's door
In pain, forgot she was so mean
She cried and knocked and knocked some more
'Please, Mole, please, quickly let me in'

'Will let you in if you promise
When you build your nest, you will care
Enough to let me see the forest
A view I know must be so fair'

 25th September

'Yes, yes, I promise,' Bird said
He let her in and nursed her wing
And saw that all her needs were met
Days later she could laugh and sing

And when Bird could fly again
She left and built a nest anew
Came back, 'Get on my back, my friend
It's time to see the forest view.'

Cheryl Gordon

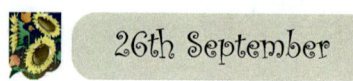

26th September

Polka-Dot, The Pony

Polka-Dot the pony was a total pampered pet.
Polka-Dot the pony, detested getting wet!
Impossible this problem, it rained an awful lot.
Only when the sun shone, would she venture out to trot.

They bought a big umbrella, with pink and purple spots.
They felt she'd much prefer it, since her name was Polka-Dot.
Next they called a factory, that made a special coat.
Waterproofed and measured, from tip of tail, to throat.

Still it proved impossible as Polka-Dot refused
To walk through muddy puddles, in her tippy-tappy shoes.
There really was no answer, but to buy her wellie boots.
They modelled them from plastic, her stable's drainpipe chutes.

This ended all the tantrums. The effort all worthwhile!
A pony in galoshes, produced a million smiles.
A genius wrote a movie, he called it *'Go and Stop'*
The star, of course, just had to be - that pony . . . Polka-Dot!

Mary Buckley-Clarke

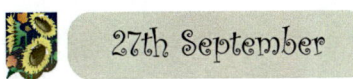

27th September

The Littlest One

Why am I always the littlest one,
the one who takes all the knocks?
Why am I always the littlest one,
the one who wears hand-me-down frocks?

My brother and sister are bigger than me,
they have large slices of cake for their tea;
because I am just the littlest one,
I have to make do with a small penny bun.
Mum, why do I have to be last?

Because I am just the littlest one,
I have to do things I hate.
Because I am just the littlest one,
they won't let me stay up late.

My brother and sister are older than me,
they have lots of secrets they won't share with me;
Because I am just the littlest one,
they shut me outside till the telling is done.
Mum, why do I have to be last?

Why did you have me the last in the line,
instead of having me first?
Why did you have me the last in the line
since last in the line comes off worst?

Peggy Netcott

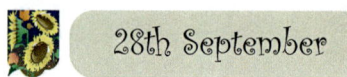 28th September

The Party

There'll be a literary party at Buckingham Palace,
Will Harry Potter be taking Alice?
With Bob the Builder and Postman Pat -
Watch out corgies for Jess the cat!
The Queen's invited the Queen of Hearts,
Perhaps she's making her famous tarts.
You may see Noddy and Paddington Bear -
The Snowman and Mawgli will both be there.
Mary Poppins and Bert the sweep,
Mr Happy and Little Bo-Peep.
Peter Pan and Toad of Toad Hall,
And many more - you'll see them all.
Two thousand children will be invited,
There'll be a huge bouncy castle to get them excited.
Working up appetites for a birthday tea,
Of sausages, ice cream and strawberry jelly.
A birthday cake made fit for a Queen -
The most beautiful cake that has ever been seen.
The Queen will be wearing her best party dress,
So learn how to curtsey if you wish to impress.
Sing 'Happy Birthday' - let out a cheer,
For our Queen celebrating her 80th year.
And when you get home, it's polite, don't you see,
To write and say 'Thank you' to Her Majesty.

Janet Fludder

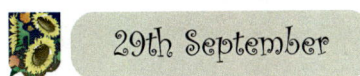

29th September

First Love

(Written for my grandson, Michael Andrews)

I wait for her every day
And also at twilight.
When she comes, my heart beats so fast.
Sometimes I am asleep
But Grandma wakes me
And throws open the door excitedly -
I search the skies . . .
I hear her first
As she roars her greeting like thunder
And I am under her spell!
She screams across the sky
Above my grandma's garden -
A slim silver delta-winged creature
Of such grace and beauty.
I gaze and gaze,
Mesmerised by her awesome power.
Was there ever such a wondrous
Supersonic sight?
I'm only five but this I know . . .
When I'm grown, my dream alone
Is to be a Concorde pilot!

Pauline Andrews

30th September

Bookworm

Little bookworm
Sitting there
On my desk
Without a care,

Would you bid me
Time of day
As I wile
My time away?

Little bookworm
Can't you see
You're such a special
Friend to me?

You listen to
My thoughts and cares
You listen while
I say my prayers.

Little bookworm
You're so bright
You seem to get
The whole lot right.

Little bookworm
As I read
Give me wisdom
To succeed!

John Henry Foley

1st October

Sad Tales Of Woe

Old Mother Gramps,
Got her kick licking stamps.
Disappeared, so the story goes,
For a harsh wind blew
A stamp to her nose;
Now she's lost in the post,
Somewhere, we hope, near you!

****

Johnny was hungry, so they all said,
So hungry was he, he went off to bed;
So hungry was Johnny, he ate off his head,
Now poor Johnny's not hungry, cos Johnny is dead!

****

'Twas Mr Ghost that ate all the toast,
But Mr Ghost being gluttonous, really fancied the roast;
So Mr Ghost thought it over: if he boast to Host
That it was he, Mr Ghost, that had ate the toast, then, he would get no roast!
So clever Mr Ghost played dumb to Host, while dishing out delicious, dripping roast,
And only then, after gulping down the thick, brown roast, began to brag and gloat,
That it be the sumptuous roast he loved the most, and of his eating of the toast,
With lashings of dripping butter, spread from coast to coast . . .
Why. . . why, why was Host
Looking mortified,
As if he'd seen some - ghost?
Then it dawned upon the horrified
Poor Mr Ghost,
After he polished off the creamy toast and after many delicious helpings of dripping roast,
Without a doubt, his poor ticker gave out, to become for sure,
A real *live* ghost.

Glenwyn Peter Evans

2nd October

Bed Bugs!

There is a monster in my closet
That hides behind the door
I know that it gets out sometimes
I've seen its footprints on my floor

I'm sure that it is scary
With fang-filled manic grin
And one day it will be waiting
For me when I get in

There is something living underneath my bed
That hides there in the day
It waits until the light goes out
And then it starts to play

It has great big claw-fingered hands
But no body to be seen
It goes in search of dangling limbs
And tugs at blankets when I dream.

Dave Palmer

3rd October

There's A Monster In My Bedroom

There's a monster in my bedroom,
It's made a mess on the floor.
There's a monster in my bedroom,
It's drawn all over the door.

There's a monster in my bedroom,
It's pulled my curtains down,
There's a monster in my bedroom,
It's wearing my dressing gown.

There's a monster in my bedroom,
It's taken the quilt off my bed.
There's a monster in my bedroom,
It's got my pants on its head.

There's a monster in my bedroom,
Mum, come quick and see.
There's a monster in my bedroom,
And that monster is . . .
Me!

Rachel Hobson

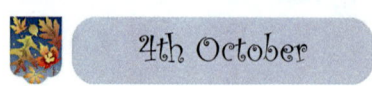

4th October

Strangers In The Night

Can you hear the strangers coming?
Coming yet so fleet
As they follow distant lines far off
Far off a search they seek
Can you hear the strangers coming by?
Clickety . . . clickety . . . clack
These nightly ghosts the stars do blink
Within the sky they pack.

Can you hear the strangers passing?
Passing in the night
As they run a beaten path laid bare
Laid bare by silver light
Can you hear the strangers passing by?
Clickety . . . clickety . . . clack
These spectral ghosts the moonlight leads
Along a silver track.

Can you hear the strangers slipping?
Slipping into dreams
Running lines the moon set down
Set down on moonlit beams
Can you hear the strangers' fading wail?
How long before they're back?
These phantom ghosts who haunt the night
Clickety . . . clickety . . . clack.

Martin James Banasko

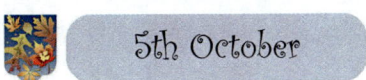

5th October

Four Years Old

She never stops talking
And even out walking
Asks questions with 'Why?' all the time,
She's bossy and tough
Plays games that are rough
And pinches her brother's green slime.

Then some days she's girlie
And wears her hair curly
With dresses of pink frills and lace,
To boys it's alarming
She can be so charming
With perfume and paint on her face.

At night when she's sleepy,
She's niggly and weepy,
Her energy's burnt to a thread,
Then cuddly and kissy
It's such a sweet missy
Who falls fast asleep in her bed.

Joy Saunders

6th October

Belinda Moon

A witch who wished she wasn't
Every potion spelled dirge and doom
A black-cat loving catastrophe
And her name? Belinda Moon . . .

Too fat to ride a broomstick,
Too blonde for Hallowe'en,
Too kind to use 'an eye of newt'
The funniest witch you've ever seen.

She was ordered to poison the village
Her cauldron bubbled for hours
But instead of many poor sick souls
Their gardens all sprung with red flowers!

'Oh shoot and shivers,' said Belinda Moon
Peering out behind her curtain
'If the black council see my useless work
I'll be de-broomed, that's certain!'

So she set to work on a really bad curse
As the stars of Hallowe'en shone bright
'Hmmm, this should set the village on fire!'
But she crossed her fingers in fright . . .

The black council rode high above
Cackling for the fun to start
But they were blown clean off their broomsticks
As a million fireworks lit the dark.

The villagers cheered at the beauty
Belinda Moon owned up, with glee;
'Don't de-broom me, I quit right now
Being a good witch is much more me!'

Danielle Eyres

The Spider

Spin, spin, spin,
Now at the light of day,
Your web is ready and waiting,
Waiting, waiting for its prey.

A butterfly alights on a flower,
A hoverfly zooms so quickly by,
While you await that fateful hour,
With gossamer ready,
To tie up your prey.

Your beady eyes watching,
Watching and waiting,
Waiting for that fateful day,
When you entice a juicy fly,
Into your web, that's hung so high.

Magdalene Chadwick

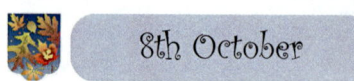

8th October

The Resident Ghost

'This house is truly haunted.'
They were talking by the door,
of scratching noises in the night,
dark shapes across the floor.

Squeaking noises in the eaves,
swift chills from ice-cold air,
a shuffling in the basement,
and a ghost upon the stairs.

But I've never seen a phantom,
and I like my empty house.
I'm glad my scratching scared them,
as I'm just a little mouse.

Kerri Fordham

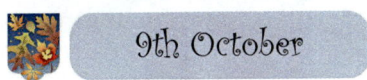

9th October

Mr Hairy Scary Legs

I'm Mr Hairy Scary Spider,
Nestling near your bed,
Now that you are sleeping,
I'll weave my sticky web.
With eight hairy, scary legs,
I'm waiting by your bed,
And if I don't trap a fly,
It might be you instead!

Sarah Ashby

10th October

Cassy The Cat

Cassy the cat was a venturesome tom,
He would climb all the trees
In the town of Random.
The roof of a house was surely the best
Like climbing Ben Nevis
It was a great conquest.
He swelled with pride to a very large size
And there he sat like
He had won first prize.
A great wind came which blew and blew,
And Cassy blew away
To Timbuktu.
The folk in the town were very sad,
And thought that Cassy
Was not so bad.
So they roamed far and wide to find Timbuktu
At last they caught sight
Of a cat they once knew.
He sat on a throne in a land of cats
You could be sure
It was free of all rats
They all set off back to sea once more
To take Cassy home to the
English seashore.
Now he sits by the winter fire
But in the dark nights
The roofs he dreams to aspire.

Joyce Gale

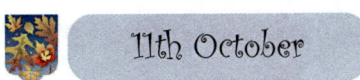

11th October

The Magic Tree

It stands in a garden of silver mist,
The leaves are damp where rain has kissed.
Heart-shaped blossoms in luminous white,
Brighten the sky with magical light.

Its trunk stands firm in shades of gold,
Names have been carved in letters bold.
Listen carefully, you'll hear the tree sing,
You might even hear the fairy bells ring.

Deep below is a purple maze
Hidden from any human gaze.
Flowers like lollipops grow in rows,
Sugar pink lanes lead where no one knows.

Inside the tree it's a secret world,
Little tree elves asleep are curled.
Their faces are green, their ears are red,
Tufts of white hair sprout out of their head.

They sleep all day and work all night,
If you are lucky you might catch sight
Of a door opening into the tree
Little elves busy making their tea.

Don't disturb them or give them a fright,
They care for our gardens through the night.
Repairing squashed daisies without a sigh,
Picking up stars that fall from the sky.

Angela Bullock

12th October

Classroom Chaos

Our classroom is in chaos,
Our teacher's going mad,
Paint and glue are everywhere,
It's looking really bad.

English books have disappeared,
Maths work's stuck to the floor,
The computer's printing out rude words,
It's never done that before.

The science topic's blown up,
Our artwork's run away,
And all the library's textbooks
Are for auction on eBay.

The head's locked in the cupboard
And can't get out - hooray!
Our classroom is in chaos,
This is such a brilliant day!

Sue Smith

13th October

The Magic Roundabout

So far away, one clear, starry night
The moon was shining so very bright
The naughty, disobedient gnome said to the goblin
'Will you go to Fairyland?' he demanded, with a grin

The goblin refused, the gnome knew he wasn't allowed
He disobediently went, and shouted out aloud
The fairies heard him and disappeared
But the fairy godmother, suddenly appeared

She waved her wand, he landed on the roundabout
He swung round and round, he started to cry, without a doubt
'I feel giddy,' he cried, she again waved her magic wand
He didn't know where he was going, and landed in a pond

The ducks were annoyed, after being awoken
And watched this peculiar figure, his nose all swollen
He must have fallen down upon underneath stones
The ducks just pecked him, well, he was full of groans

'I can't swim,' he cried, waking the swans up too
They were annoyed with the gnome, who didn't know what to do
The gnome had had enough of the pecks, and strange water
The fairy godmother aimed her wand, at this terrible creature

He pinched a pixie's wing, behind the fairy godmother's back
The ducks watched and gave a very loud quack
The pixie screamed, and flew on one wing
Well, the disobedient gnome had had his fling

The fairy godmother whisked him back, to the goblin's homestead
Wondering if he will go back to Fairyland, well, I begin to dread
Children, if you ever see a pixie, with her wing so bruised
Or if you ever see a magic roundabout, just be amused

You may not see the fairies dance, through the night
Because, children, you should be in your beds, sleeping tight.

Jean McGovern

Jockwin The Goblin

This tale is about Jockwin the goblin
A goblin as you know is a tiny wee man
And he loves to practise his magic
As the very best goblins all can

He lived deep in the green forest
In a fairy house by a stream
Happy and safe in the knowledge that
By humans he couldn't be seen

When the local children came to play
And sometimes trampled his fence to the ground
He'd get angry and, to get his own back
Scare them off by making wild animal sounds

Or he would magic the trees to reach out for them
As they ran here and there at their play
And as the branches would reach out and clutch at their legs
They'd scream in terror and run fast away

As they would run in fear from the forest
He would chase them though they couldn't see
But they would hear his hysterical laughter
As he would caper and dance in his glee

But then when the forest was quiet once more
And just the sound of the birds filled the air
He'd get lonely and long for a visit
Of the children that once more he could scare.

Don Woods

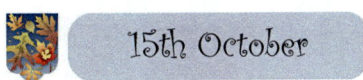
15th October

The Very Thin Boy

You are so very thin, boy,
Your thinness is something queer;
Were you to stand behind a lamp post
You'd simply disappear.

You really ought to eat more
And fill your tum like us,
For who could fail to spot us?
We're like the back end of a bus.

From drains and pipes and holes and such
You really should stand back,
For if you fell down any of these
We'd never get you back.

And do not stand too near a fence
That's half-built at the most:
They'll likely nail the crossbars to you
Thinking you're a post!

And when you go into the sea,
Be sure your swimming's good:
Someone might think you're a floating log
And chop you up for wood.

And do not bend into the wind too much
To shield you from its racket:
Some DIY freak well might nab you
And use you for a bracket.

The boy, grown tired of this, then realised
Why they spoke to him like that:
'It's not that I'm so very thin,' he cried,
'It's because you're all so *very fat!*'

Philip Sanders

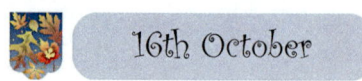 16th October

The Noise

(For Alannah)

Is it a road drill, digging up the road
or the mating call of a giant toad?
No, it's Grandad snoring.

Is it thunder - there's no lightning in the sky -
or a pterodactyl learning how to fly?
No, it's Grandad snoring.

Is it a jumbo jet rumbling through a cloud
or a fast train passing? It's very, very loud.
No - just Grandad snoring.

Catherine Bradbury

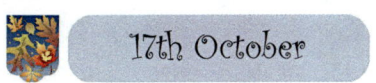
17th October

Ambrose, The Cat, Up A Tree

Here I am, up this very nice big tree,
The whole wide world looking up at me,
From here, I can see any window or door,
If I move up higher, I can see even more,
The wind blows my fur all over the place,
And my whiskers all around my furry face,
I'm really not too skinny, and not too fat,
In fact, I am quite a fit and healthy cat,
I hope it doesn't rain, and I get all soggy,
I don't want to be a soaking wet moggy,
If it snows, I will turn white and freeze,
My black fur will shiver and I will sneeze,
Holding onto this branch, with each claw,
To fall off the tree, even gravity has a law,
A very bright sun shines down on me,
Me, a happy cat sitting here on this tall tree,
A small bird singing right above me, I heard,
Oh how annoying, what a noisy little bird,
A big dog is barking at me down below, I fear,
But I'm not really scared, I'm safe up here,
A man on a motorbike is speeding past,
How is he peddling and cycling so fast?
A church nearby, where tombstones grace,
This churchyard is a very grave place,
It's time for me to come down from this tree,
As there is some food waiting at home for me!

Christopher Higgins

18th October

Mad Cat

I sat on the wall and what did I see?
Our marmalade cat up in the tree
He looked down at me with a whimsical stare
His back legs sticking straight up in the air.

I wondered how did he get like that
This ridiculous, adventurous, marmalade cat
Mad acrobatics in the chestnut tree
When he could be purring on my knee.

'Swan Lake' can't hold a candle to him
He must be attending the local gym
Wow, now his tail is pointing straight out
Do you think he will fall if I give him a shout?

Paws all aquiver, he straddles a twig
He looks like a pantomime dame in a wig
Next thing I know, he's spotted a bird
No, he can't be stalking it, that's just absurd.

Yes, he thinks he can reach it, he's having a ball
But, oh dear, I think he's in a free fall
Oh how I love him, this bundle of fun
Orange fur standing on end in the sun.

Tumbling down bat-like, with legs stretched out wide
I'm laughing so much, I've a stitch in my side
The bird makes an exit as fast as a rocket
No time to put marbles back in my pocket
My poor dear sweet kitty, is nearing the ground
But would you believe it, he makes not one sound!

So that is the story of our marmalade cat
I thought he would hit the ground with a splat
But he sailed through the air with the greatest of ease
Then walked up the path, with just one *mighty sneeze* . . .

Jennifer H Fox

19th October

Fun In The Rain

There are lots of puddles in the road and in my garden too
And puddles on the pavement and now they're in my shoe
I jumped and landed in this one, I thought it would be fun
But now my feet and socks are wet and squelch when I run.

Whilst standing at the bus stop, I am in such wild delight
The traffic splashes all the folk, they do look such a sight
I'm lucky I am at the back, no splashes here catch me
Mum can't be mad at me now, for she's wet as wet can be.

Umbrellas jogging down the street, every colour, size and shape
Some have spokes that stick right out, it is a funny jape
They twist and twirl or flap and flutter, in the wind they bellow
I even saw one being chased by a bowler-hatted fellow.

If I stick my tongue out and turn my face up to the sky
I can feel the raindrops landing, you could do it if you try
It's good to have some fun with rain, it stops you feeling sad
And maybe if we laugh at it instead, we could all feel glad.

Jean Selmes

20th October

Wizard

I'm sure you know someone who's got a book about young Harry Potter.
The Royal Mail will surely scowl at post delivered by an owl.
When playing Quidditch on a broom make sure that you've got flying room.
You'll need to get an armoured tank to crack the vaults at Gringott's Bank
but you'll need gold to get all pally with salesmen in Diagon Alley.
It's not the back of beyond, it's where you go to buy a wand,
an owl or bat, or something similar, you'll need to have as a 'familiar'.
Why all these things? Ah, can't you guess? It's when you catch Hogwarts Express.
In weather fine, or in a blizzard, you go to learn to be a wizard.
And though it is a hearty struggle, you will learn far more than a muggle
who lives a dull suburban life with dull fat kids and a dull thick wife.
Now wizards can have lots of fun, they use their wands to conjure sun
and when they want to go away, they use their broomsticks not BA!
A good 2000, flying high, can beat most aircraft in the sky.
So wizards, when they go abroad, use their broomsticks - not a Ford.

D G W Garde

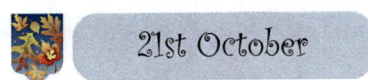

Potion To Make A Brother Disappear

Take some hair from his head
Take a cup of dribble while he's asleep in bed
Take lots of bogeys from his nose
Take a nail clipping from both big toes

Take two slugs and one snail
Mush it all up in a black pail
Take some sticks and some stones
Take some really old bones

Grind them small, then mix it all well
Add water slowly to help it gel
Put in something he will really fear
That's how to make a brother disappear!

Carrie-Anne Fry

 22nd October

Sarah

Sarah was quite a brainy girl, no one ever knew just why
Always getting marks at school, marks ever, oh, so high
Sarah, she was a quiet girl but was also a secret magician
Joined the Harry Potter Fan Club, their latest yet addition
Now she was using her magic to make her brainy too
And help improve her magic skill, I would, wouldn't you?
But too much magic in one go made her bounce about
Bursting to get out of her, it jumped without any doubt
Every time it bounced inside, she flew through the air
Puzzled frowns upon her face showed her sad despair
But Harry Potter heard of this and came to her rescue
For no one else in the fan club had known just what to do
Harry looked at Sarah, gave a wink, kissed her on the cheek
Sarah felt her knees indeed buckle as they went all weak
Harry had sucked the magic out, leaving in just enough
She bounced with joy, hit the roof, her head was really tough
Bounced not because of the magic, but her heart had leapt
Meeting Harry Potter you see, a wish, she had always kept.

C R Slater

23rd October

Nursery Magic

The children have all gone to bed and everything is quiet
And then the nursery clock strikes eight and the silence comes apart.
The lady on the music box begins her dainty dance
And the little rocking horse starts to prance.

The dollies in the doll's house make sandwiches with cheese
Then invite the soldiers from the fort to come in and share their tea.
The big brown bear and the Indian chief decide to have a race
The brown bear wins as the chief falls flat upon his face.

Skittles climb upon the train as it chuffs along the rails
While Postman Pat is busy sorting out his mail.
The building bricks have made an arch for the toy cars to go through
Then Neddy, the woollen donkey, decides that he'll go too.

The bats and balls play cricket upon the carpet which is green
The larger dolls all watch them, it makes a lovely scene.
Outside a blackbird starts to sing to herald a new day
There's quite a bit of rushing about and the toys are all away.

J H Jenkins

24th October

Brand New Train Set

A brand new train set, a birthday surprise!
I can't believe what's here before my eyes
The smile on my face, it's from ear to ear
A whistle blows; we all let out a cheer!

The kids from the street, they're all gathering around
All staring at my train, they're not making a sound
Some want to touch it, *don't* you dare!
It nearly comes off the track. Ohh! What a scare!

There's only one thing wrong that I can see
This beautiful train set, doesn't really belong to me!
Dad's hogging all the fun, the remote he grasps
'How long is this test run, Dad, going to last?

Come on Dad, *please!* Can I have a go?'
This father of mine is really putting on quite a show!
He says, 'Not yet, son, I've got to get it right!'
I don't think my turn's anywhere in sight!

All the kids are staring at me and my dad
They all know the feeling, we've all been had
Golly gosh! Dad's finally handing me the remote!
Ahh! The batteries are dead! *You old goat!*

Russell Harvey Mortimer

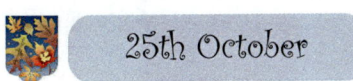

The Haunted House

There's a haunted house at the end of our road,
With hardly any windows,
I'm scared to pass it after dark,
Especially when the wind blows.

A gravel path leads up to the door,
Which once was painted grey.
The gates are tied together with string,
And the posts have rotted away.

There's a cypress hedge at the end of the lawn,
Which is now a tangle of weeds,
Brambles grow across the porch
Where a solitary sycamore seeds.

But someone must be living there,
You can see a light at night,
Yet I've never seen a living soul -
But one of these days I might!

I sometimes see a Siamese cat,
Which is too peculiar for words.
It lies in the overgrown porch all day
And scares off all the birds.

Something terrible happened there,
I can feel it in my bones,
But no one knows now what it was -
Except those crumbling stones.

John Coombes

26th October

Moon's Naughty Kittens

Moon the cat had kittens three:
Merlin, Star and Zebedee.
They all belonged to Old Ma Nell,
A witch who brewed a mean old spell.

She swept the house, to make it clean
For party night on Hallowe'en.
The kittens chased her wooden broom,
And followed her from room to room.

She thought that she would take a nap,
With Moon asleep upon her lap.
The kittens, though, were wide awake,
And full of mischief they could make.

They pounced on Old Nell's sweeping brush,
And flew up quickly, in a rush!
They all clung on in fear and fright,
Across the skies, that autumn night.

Then Nell woke up to Moon's miaow,
She had to get them home somehow.
She waved her wand, 'Come back you kits!'
The broom crashed down and fell to bits.

'No treats for you!' the old witch cried,
'I've got no magic broom to ride!'
They hung their heads, and shed a tear,
'We won't fly off again, no fear!'

Brenda Maple

27th October

Ghastly Grime

Wash your hands!
Clean your teeth!
Scrub those ghastly,
smelly feet!
Brush your hair!
Do your nails!
Is that a tidemark
or the sails?
Oh, those knees
black with grime.
Elbows thick with
frogspawn slime.
Wipe your nose!
Not on your sleeve!
With a tissue,
if you please.
No, don't pick it!
Blow or sneeze,
discreetly, nicely
so no one sees.
Into the bath
before your bed!
There is no more
to be said!
Ah, fresh and clean,
sweet and pink.
No longer ponging
of kitchen sink.

Janet M Pinto

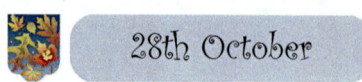

28th October

Hallowe'en Magic

H allowe'en is upon us
A special magic is unleashed
L ock all your doors and windows
L unacy reigns supreme
O ld hags in black dresses
W eave their spells and charms
E ven ghosts and ghoulies
E ndeavour to cause alarm
N aughty elves and pixies

M anage to cause strife
A night that's full of mischief
G iving a show of eternal life
I ncredible and empowering
C an you feel the magic too?

For I'm the King of Beasties
And I'm coming to get you!

Donna Salisbury

 29th October

Hallowe'en

(For Pauline)

On this night all witches fly
Bound for eldritch revelry;
Bats and vampires fill the air,
Sable cats prowl from their lair;
Toads and vipers roam the wood,
Owls' weird screeches freeze the blood;
Churchyards yawn, ghosts wander wide -
Fearful mortals - hark, and hide.
Yet once upon a time there stood
Round a cradle, fairies good,
On this day, and wove a charm
To ward off evil, spare from harm:
To a fairy-tale princess
And her prince, their lives to bless,
Gave a little daughter fair,
Blue of eye and gold of hair.
See her now as one more year
She has joyed her parents dear,
Grown in beauty, rich in mirth -
Happy stars beamed on her birth.

Now to all the saints we pray
Who tomorrow light the day:
Protect and keep this precious child,
Her father kind, her mother mild.

**N D Wood (Giddy great aunt, age 85,
3 times 1st Prize witch at Hallowe'en balls)**

30th October

Ode To October

Oh October, how I love thee
With your autumnal colours
Of russet-brown, amber and gold
And your bare-branched trees,
The way Jack Frost paints your grass
With a silver-tipped pen,
And silken webs glisten so delicately
As they dance in winter's breath.
You are the jewel in the seasonal crown,
Bright and mysterious
Fresh and interesting
Oh wonderful October, how I love thee so!

Lynsey Hawkins

31st October

Arctic Fox In Scarlet Socks

An Arctic fox in scarlet socks goes walking every day
And when he walks he stops and talks to friends along the way.

A polar bear with ginger hair - (he scorched it in the sun)
Just daren't go out, folks laugh and shout. They're always making fun.

But Arctic Fox has solved all that. He's brought his friend a scarlet hat.
Come on, Bear, a hat to wear. Now let's go out and take the air.

Husky Dog is needing help. He cannot bark or even yelp.
His throat's so sore he feels quite ill. So Arctic Fox gives him a pill.

But just for fun and truth to tell, he brings a scarlet scarf as well.
So Husky Dog can take the air with Arctic Fox and Polar Bear.

Reindeer Ron's a sorry sight. He's lost his antlers in a fight
And when those mighty antlers fell he lost his confidence as well.

He left the tundra long ago, now feels inadequate and low.
But Arctic Fox can help him too. 'I've brought a scarlet cloak for you.

It has a hood to hide your head. Come out with us. We're all in red.'
So Arctic Fox in scarlet socks and Polar Bear with ginger hair (and a hat on top)

Join Reindeer Ron in scarlet cloak and Husky Dog who's cured his throat
With scarlet scarf wrapped round and round. All set off, they're outward bound.

They make a warm and rosy glow as four go walking in the snow.
Friends all smile and say hello. No one jeers or sneers or mocks.
All thanks to Fox in scarlet socks.

Kay Jones

1st November

The Little White Kitten

The wind it was a-howling
When I went out to see
When this small white paper bag
Came crawling up to me

It let out a miaow
'Twas then that I could see
It was a little kitten
So I closed the door
I don't like cats, you see

I was not for admittin'
This kitten, so appealing
But I gave it milk
And scraps of bread
Then promptly I went off to bed

The next night on my doorstep
The kitten, it was there
The snow had started falling
I knew I shouldn't care
It was not my problem
As far as I could see
But this white fluffy bundle
It had adopted me

I scooped it from my doorstep
And brought the cat inside
'You can only stay a few hours
My home it is my pride
I don't want you, kitten
Messing up my home
As soon as it stops snowing
We'll go and find your home'

1st November

A year has passed, well, slightly more
My house, it has been sold
Everything is packed and on its way
To my new abode
I'm off to France tomorrow
A new life for me, you see
Well I suppose you've guessed . . .
A big white cat is coming to France with me!

Pauline Giffen

 2nd November

Who's Scared?

Who's scared of things in the night
that jump out at you and give you a fright?
Who's scared of the monster under the bed
who grabs and gobbles up your favourite ted?
Who's scared of the sock-eating beast
who at twelve every night has a sock-eating feast?
Who's scared of the bogeyman?
Dancing all night is his favourite plan.
Who's scared of wolves who will soon
be out in the dark howling at the moon?
Who's scared of witches and black cats
or sounds like the bangs and ratatat-tats?
Who's scared of vampire bats,
zombies, spiders, snakes or rats?

Not me, not my, not myself, not I
I'm not scared, what's that? 'Oh my!'
There's a bang on the door
and scratching on the floor.
'Ahhhhhh' outside someone screams.
I'm not scared, it's not what it seems.
It's not that scary, I think you will find
most of the time it's just tricks on your mind.

Ashleigh Rice (13)

3rd November

The Sleepover

'Listen,' I said, can you hear him?' as we sat up and listened intently on our bed
We held our breath, kept very close, our hearts beating with dread

We stood bare, we stood frightened, my parents safe downstairs
I could hear them talking, I could hear their programme, all completely unawares

John said he heard a rustling. Pete thought he heard something drag
Then we all saw all kinds of shadows not far away from John's overnight bag.

I tried a show of bravery, it would be different tomorrow night
But for now I had two friends as we mocked our spectre in the pale lamplight.

John whispered he saw a demon, he said he could hear the ghosts from Hell
We all froze as we heard the eleven o'clock church bell

Pete whispered that by the wardrobe he heard movement
We jumped at every bump inside and around this night

We then saw shadows form menacing shapes
In all sorts of unnatural angles from my corner bedside light

All of us kept watch and were all so very far from the land of sleep
Pete hid under his blanket, even daring the occasional peep

We three friends united, we three friends so brave, we three friends together
We three bravely kept our sleepless watch, holding hands we swore our oath,
we three friends forever

Steve Prout

4th November

Wishing Star

Does anybody know what lies
inside a wishing star?
I'd go and have a look myself
if it were not so far.
But wishing stars hang big and bright
so far above the Earth
that nobody can reach them
to find out what they're worth.

Can anybody *guess* what lies
inside a wishing star?
I think it's full of wishes
that only got that far.
I think that when it's very full
some wishes tumble out
and they're the ones that *do* come true
the ones we shout about.

If somehow I could reach it
hanging high above my town
I'd tip that star right over
'til the wishes shimmered down.
And they would fall upon the world
like sparkling drops of dew
and everyone would get a wish
and each wish would come true!

Carol Don Ercolano (New Zealand author)

 5th November

Flynn's Night Out

An adventurous little hedgehog named Flynn
went roaming one very dark night
stumbling over an empty baked bean tin
he crawled inside and got stuck really tight
Flynn wriggled and squirmed to get back out
but the can began moving and rolling about
over and over it quickly went
until Flynn felt dizzy, battered and bent
the tin suddenly came to a crashing halt
against a big tree with a sickening jolt
Flynn was flung out, thrown like a stone
fell on his feet and limped slowly home
where tucked up safely and snug in his bed
he gladly dreamed of exploring instead.

Anne Mitchell

6th November

Uncle Ted

My Uncle Ted is an inventor
He invents all kinds of stuff
He always tries his very best
But it's just not good enough

You see they all go wrong
Some of them even explode
Like the jet pack for Granny
To help her cross the road

Then we thought we had lost him
He vanished for a day or two
Uncle Ted was stuck in his room
Sitting in his glue

The last time I saw Uncle Ted
He was driving in a race
Using his new rocket fuel
Now he is lost in space.

Richard Mills

 7th November

The Door In The Floor

Where could it lead to, this door in the floor?
An enchanted kingdom, six days at war?
Genies and giants, fairies and gnomes
Battling evil from dazzling domes,
Keeping the Prince of Darkness at bay
Preserving the light from frightful decay?

Where could it lead to, this door in the floor?
To a candy land with pleasures galore?
Rivers of chocolate, jelly bean flowers
Streets of liquorice, milkshake showers,
Candyfloss clouds and candy cane trees
With orders to eat as much as you please?

Where could it lead to, this door in the floor?
To a paradise island with a golden shore?
Caves filled to the brim with pirates' treasure
Rubies and emeralds, gold for your pleasure,
Diamonds and pearls that glint in the sun
Yours for the taking after the battle you won?

Where could it lead to, this door in the floor?
To a land where worries don't exist anymore?
Where children can bounce on the clouds till they drop
Slide down the rainbow and climb to the top,
Visit the moon just to taste the cheese
Swing on the stars like a flying trapeze?

Where could it lead to, this door in the floor?
Think of the place you'd most adore,
That's where it leads to, this door in the floor!

Belinda Abraham

8th November

Do You Want To Be A Superhero?

Do you want to be a superhero,
and have lots of superpowers?
To fly from roof to roof,
or wear your pants over your trousers?

Wouldn't it be cool to drive a Batmobile,
and fly from place to place?
To rescue damsels from burning buildings,
and be gone without a trace?

Would you like to be The Hulk
and have thick green monster skin?
Or own a cape like Superman,
and have a large heroic grin?

What about some spidery senses,
wouldn't that be fun?
Or stretch, shoot fire, turn invisible,
or even fly around the sun?

If you decide to be a superhero,
those bad guys don't have a chance.
So stand up tall and say aloud -
'Mum, where are my clean pants?'

Kirsty Louise Phillips

Caring Hands

She licks my fingers
one by one
with her rough tongue
then falls asleep
on my hand.
A warm touch
comforting
as Mother Nature
gave her
when bonded
to her mother
broken all too soon.
When left to
fend for herself with none
to provide food, shelter and love.
When found by caring hands
given a chance to love
and be loved.

Peacefully she sleeps
a contented kitten.
I rest
and appreciate her beauty
now she dreams in her sleep
jumping and twitching
playing in the fields maybe
as now she dares.
But once she came out
only into the night.

Connie Moseley

10th November

A Silly Cat Called Jeremiah

A silly cat called Jeremiah
Loved to sit beside the fire
This silly cat he never learned
Was always getting his whiskers burned
One day while snoozing on the mat
Alas this very silly cat
Got too close to the open fire
And things became a little dire
Not just his whiskers did he scorch
His whole body he did torch
And now old silly Jeremiah
Has to sit beside the fire
This silly cat who you could not warn
Has no fur to keep him warm.

Trudy Simpson

11th November

Tracey Treacle

Tracey Treacle wasn't evil, just misunderstood
She didn't treat her brother, Tom, in quite the way she should
She didn't know that flicking bogies at her mum was bad
At least she didn't roll them up and eat them like her dad

Tracey Treacle wasn't evil, just misunderstood
She thought it fine to swap Tom's biscuit for a piece of wood
She got told off when she went to church without her brand new hat on
Oh no, instead, upon her head she'd superglued the cat on

Tracey Treacle wasn't evil, just misunderstood
She thought that she was normal and sometimes even good
She thought it cool to close the gate before her gran walked through it
And that was even after Mum had told her not to do it

Tracey Treacle wasn't evil, just misunderstood
She didn't mean to put Gran's teeth inside the Christmas pud
She wasn't sure the kids next door would find it rather rude
When she clambered over the garden fence and ate their rabbit's food

Tracey Treacle wasn't evil, just misunderstood
She just got bored of doing things like all the others would
She had a laugh when in Dad's bath she threw her new pet toad
It swam about and Dad hopped out, and the bath, it overflowed.

Graeme Illingworth

12th November

Impasse

A rabbit, hopping down the road,
Espied a frog (or was it a toad?)
Sitting, pondering, deep in thought,
Eating a fly he'd recently caught.
The rabbit, now his path was barred,
Thought very long and very hard,
And said to the frog (or was it a toad?)
'Dear Sir (or Madam), you're in my road.'
The frog (or toad) blinked his eyes,
Croaked loud, and sounded very wise,
'You stupid rabbit (or are you a hare?),
What you are I do not care.
With your long legs, you can hop
Above my head, so do not stop,
Leave me alone to eat my fly,
So off you go and pass me by.
The rabbit (hare) was very confused,
In fact, he seemed to be bemused.
How could a frog (or was it a toad?)
Stop him from hopping down the road?
He slowly turned and walked away
To tell his friends about his day.
To be called a rabbit or maybe a hare
Was more than a rabbit could really bear!

Edward S Wall

13th November

Granny's Pantry

My granny has a room called a pantry,
With shelves full of packets and jars.
It's got enough food and drink stored there,
To last the long journey to Mars!
The last time I stayed overnight there,
Lying warm and tucked up in my bed,
The sounds of shrill voices and singing,
Buzzed round and around in my head.
I sat up and thought I was dreaming,
But the noises were real, that was clear,
So I decided to investigate further,
And see what it was I could hear.
I tiptoed down into the kitchen,
A light shone 'neath the old pantry door,
I opened it just a wee fraction,
And couldn't believe what I saw!
The jam jars were doing a foxtrot,
The cornflakes were dancing a jig,
The Coke cans were playing a calypso,
An orange spun around with a fig!
It seemed like the whole house was jumping,
When I thought I heard somebody call,
Then it was quiet again in the pantry,
It was maybe a dream after all!
I turned and saw Granny behind me,
Her eyes twinkled with a magical glow,
She asked me to keep it a secret,
So please don't let on that you know!

David Anderson

14th November

Among The Clover

At the bottom of my garden
Lives a tiny little lad
I know you won't believe me
And you'll think that I am mad

His clothes are bright and colourful
Scarlet-red and emerald-green
He has the pointiest of feet
That I have ever seen

He wears a little black top hat
Upon his head of orange hair
And he sits among the clover
With a petal for a chair

I don't know where he came from
Or how long that he will stay
But I know I'll miss the little lad
If he has to go away

I think he is a leprechaun
Or a pixie of some kind
But who this little lad is
I really do not mind

I do not mind him sitting there
He doesn't do me any harm
He said that he can bring me luck
So he is my lucky charm

At the bottom of the garden
Lives a tiny little lad
Please come and take a look yourself
Then you'll know that I'm not mad.

Julie L Preston

15th November

Magical Carpet

Onward and over,
Through the night sky.
Deep valley, tall mountain,
Blue seas flashing by.

Into the night,
The world whistles by.
Magical carpet
High up in the sky.

With colours of green,
White, red and yellow,
Gasps of surprise
From the people below.

Into the distance,
Still heading on,
Magically shrinking,
Magically gone!

Colin Wallace

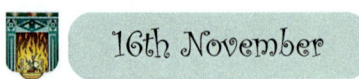

16th November

Cupcakes For A Crocodile

In a quiet area in Africa, there lived a grumpy crocodile
A long-tailed dirty creature that would never smile
His home was on the riverbank where he slept all day in the sun
Sometimes he'd cool off in the muddy waters, but never splash or have fun

This large reptile had thick, crumbly skin, coloured brown and green
With flaking bits and blotches of sand and grime in-between
He didn't join the crocodiles at the other end of the river
He had scary dark eyes that could make you shiver

He didn't talk to the playful hippos, not even the slimy eels
And only left his home when he heard fishermen's reels
He didn't hunt ducks or eat any meat at all
Croc was a vegetarian, from the day he learnt to crawl

He enjoyed eating leaves, stems, petals and bark
And would search for wild berries at night in the dark
But something was missing from his veggie diet
There was no flavour, that really caused him a riot

Until one day, a family settled nearby for their picnic lunch
The smell of their food made crocodile want to munch
He was intrigued by an unfamiliar sweet smell
A hint of vanilla, perhaps caramel, he just couldn't tell

He crept towards them and tried to hide behind a rock
They screamed when they saw him and ran away in shock
He examined their meal, now scattered all over the lawn
While sniffing sandwiches, his mouth opened wide like a yawn

Then he smelled sugar, almost drowned by the sun
While he tasted what looked like a round, iced bun
He gobbled up all the others till there were none left to eat
And crocodile decided he preferred cupcakes to meat.

Atiyah Wazir

 17th November

Birds Of Prey

Freddie was a field vole, no bigger than your thumb,
Who played upon wasteland where the pylons would hum,
On grassy embankments or the odd garden plot.
Said he felt quite at home in his upturned plant pot.

Fay, too, was a field vole, the idol of his eye.
He met her in the barley where the knot they did tie.
She wanted the country but that brought on a frown
For he was quite settled on the edge of the town.

Kenny was a kestrel with a keen appetite.
He would perch on flyovers or hover like a kite.
From his best vantage point on top of the mill,
If he saw something move, he was in for the kill!

Ivor was a tawny owl who saw better at night.
He would close but one eye when the prey was in sight,
Then turn his head sideways, he'd take aim and swoop.
Much squawking and flapping as a morsel he'd scoop.

I remember the day the field voles broke cover,
As I sat by the stream with Gladys, my lover.
They ran to the sunshine to get out of the shade
And Kenny and Ivor saw the table was laid.

One from east, one from west, they both dived from on high.
The air seemed so silent as they zoomed through the sky,
With eyeballs locked on and wings built to precision,
They swooped, how they swooped to a head-on collision.

As for Freddie and Fay who were both unaware,
Of their lucky escape from the birds in the air,
They just could not decide between country and town,
And they still chewed the fat 'til the whole sun went down.

Bernard Brady

18th November

Three Million, Two Hundred And Two Weeks Ago

Last night I was told a story and I want you all to know
About a dinosaur and his family; it happened many long years ago
The dinosaur was grazing by a swamp; lazily chewing his cud
Looking down past some trees, into the musty, bubbling mud

The dinosaur was happy and nothing did he fear
Suddenly from that swamp, some bubbles did appear
As he watched that swamp, it bubbled madly and then
First there was one and, before he knew it, there were ten

Those bubbles moved together; suddenly they became just one
That dinosaur shook his head and looked up at the morning sun
Thinking that his father had told him, many years before
That his father had seen this, but thought it just folklore

I better check this out, so he moved a little more near
Now from that swamp, more and more bubbles did appear
Again they moved together, like he had seen in the past
Lazily chewing a branch from a tree, knowing this would not last

But thousands of bubbles did appear, and now they moved to ground
As that dinosaur looked he did find, hundreds more were all around
Then as the sun began to rise, those large bubbles shed their skin
How was that poor dinosaur to know, that mankind was to begin?

He looked at the far and distant sea and there he saw many,
Many more
Suddenly more and more bubbles were coming fast to distant shore
The dinosaur looked at his family; he gazed at them with pride
How was that dinosaur to know, more bubbles coming in
With each tide?

Now those bubbles had shapes and some even moved into
A small huddle
Those new creatures were now drinking, from a large new puddle
Oh how was that poor dinosaur to know that Man's time had begun?

 18th November

The dinosaur began to laugh, he knew he would not be here for long
For those bubbles now dancing, could it be, they were singing
An Irish song?

Yes, that is the story I was told, as I lay sick in my bed
It is the story true of Ireland, and that is what my grandad
Has just said.

F K McGarry

Manosaur

Up in the hills I heard a roar
Not man, not beast, but Manosaur
I waited in my climbing shoes
To see if I could glimpse a view
The sky, it blackened over me
Cagoule hood up and all ready

To hunt the monster of the mount
With bated breath I then did count
My footsteps as I neared to him
Did creep and goosebumps reached my skin
When suddenly at once I stopped
I spied a claw beside a rock

I looked on speechless and in awe
Could this belong to Manosaur?
It snorted and sensed I was there
I screamed and ran from my brave dare
Back to my home far from the green
Where Manosaurs are never seen.

D M Brighton

20th November

Snail-Trail Tale

This is the tale - of the trail - of a snail
 which led - like a thread - to a shed
  where a skunk - slunk - on a bunk
   was deep - in a heap - fast asleep
    in a dream of an ice cream stream!
     What a sight - in the night - pure delight!
     thought the skunk - slunk - on a bunk!
  I'll follow my nose - and see where it goes - so he rose
  from his nest and - with zest - got dressed -
 to follow the ice cream dream stream.
Sniffing its scent - head bent - off he went -
 our sure-footed rover - over the clover
  into the night - by the light of the bright
   silver moon, but his tune soon
    changed when the stream didn't seem to be like ice cream:
     no, it wasn't quite right - not at all milky white
     but more of a mellow yellow - poor fellow
   he took one lick of the slick and was sick!
  Bad lad! Rather sad - for what had
  before (he was sure) been an ice cream was no more
than the pale, pallid trail of a snail
 which led - like a thread- to a shed
  where a skunk - slunk - on a bunk
   was deep - in a heap - fast asleep
    in a dream of an ice cream stream.

Alan Millard

21st November

The Benefit Of Bedtime Books

Ages ago and in a far distant land
Kids stayed up all night for no sleep was at hand
Their mothers and fathers could never see why
But they sang and they sang such a long lullaby
All night they would sing but never a wink
Of sleep for the kids not an eyelid would blink
Exhausted at last they said, it's absurd
A problem like this has never been heard
Strange potions and pills do not make them sleep
But they found in the corner some books in a heap
Books full of stories up to now were ignored
But reading them slowly they soon will be bored
The solution was there at the time soporific
With long words, yes long words - effective, terrific!
Inexhaustible slumber - the sleep metaphor
You can't hear the kids - so loud is the snore!

Gerald S Bell

 22nd November

Bedtime Grime

Come along, it's bedtime -
First the bath, clean the grime
Pull the plug, watch the slime
Gurgle down the hole in time
Now standing up and out you climb
Towel working overtime
Old pyjamas green as lime.

Come along, it's bedtime -
Hear the big old hall clock chime?
Shouting out, 'It's night-time'
Now into bed, and up you climb
Too tired to play pantomime
But I'll sing your favourite nursery rhyme
Just one more time.

Lorelei Long

23rd November

Blackbird

New little blackbird
Sitting all alone
Fluff up your feathers
And then go home

New little blackbird
Wait until the spring
Then we can hear
Your silver voice sing

New little blackbird
Make yourself a nest
Fill it with songbirds
Summer is the best

Hey little blackbird
Now you're not so new
Sing your way to winter
Now that autumn's through.

Christine Renee Parker

24th November

Pie-Eyed

Visits up to Yorkshire yearly,
I missed when I grew up dearly,
minced beef pies the motive clearly.

We'd travel five hours in the car,
always getting lost and counting stars,
fireflies humming on air guitars.

My auntie was an alien,
dimples as large as currant buns,
a northern lingo and bunions.

My auntie had bold, child-bearing hips,
always wore clothes too tight to fit but
baked savoury pies: a joy to lips.

Jackie was a lass, no madame,
she sliced *Spam* or made her jam;
yet her pies pursued the grand slam!

Claret-crayoned skies, hot beef pies,
northern wind bullies tears from eyes,
I, some soft southerner hypnotised.

Stone Roses syllable streamed
from the kitchen radio beams,
Morrissey's mumblings cooked up dreams.

Her warm larder (everything fried),
those home-cooked pies were worth the ride,
worth the travel-sick journey despised.

Thankful for pastry family ties;
oh! I love the northern vibes!
Sharp winds, sharp music and the pies.

Sarah Louise Parry

One Night

The night sits black in musty blues,
'Be patient,' says the voice of the silver-laced moon.
'Tonight the lake of frosty green,
Plays our host of a most magical scene.'
Out dance the stars in a milky trance,
Lighting the little lake with energy that sparks.
Electric shimmers off the rising golden forks,
Give way to the King of Waters, Triton, as he talks,
'On this dreamy night, let the mystery begin,
Come alive little myths of the sea, splash and sing,
For tonight you are free.'
Out they rose, the most peculiar of sorts,
If you had seen them, you'd have thought the most strangest of thoughts!
A beautiful mermaid scaled in gold,
Her hair a-flowing in the breeze of the cold.
Then a starfish made of solid sand,
Waggled his pink-shaded stretchy hands.
The sea horse draped in seaweed wax,
Aquamarine charm lined his tiny prickled back.
Seashelled crab of vibrant red,
Covered in silky stones from pincer to head.
Lastly, in a bottle lay an eel of yellow,
Floating with a message guarded by his tail.
The enchanted six pirouetted the rippled lake,
Singing melodies and harmonies they had made.
Rhythms of the waters brought magic to their hearts,
But the night was nearly over and the twinkling stars began to part.
And, as if by a spell, the lake vanished out of sight,
Mysteries may fade, but magic always burns bright.

Anna Green

26th November

Owl

Tu-whit, tu-whoo,
The owl does say,
At the closing of each day,
The other birds then fly away,
To where they sleep and rest.
Tu-whit, tu-whoo,
The owl does call,
Through the trees so straight and tall,
As moon does rise and sun does fall,
Slowly in the west.
Tu-whit, tu-whoo,
The owl does cry,
So graceful through the night does fly,
Without a sound its eyes do pry,
And scan the woodland floor.
Tu-whit, tu-whoo,
The owl does sing,
As to its branch it now does bring,
A tiny vole upon the wing,
And through the air does soar.

A Blakemore

27th November

Wind Man

(An ancient Scandinavian legend)

> The Wind Man dwells beyond the hill,
> The Wind Man dwells beyond the plain,
> But listen, you can hear his sound -

The Wind Man, with his paddles whirling round!

Who makes the dried red berries skitter-scatter,
Disturbs the leaves exhaling on the ground?
Who makes the wiry treetops mesh or quiver?

The Wind Man, when his paddles whirl around!

His eyes shut tight, with winter on his mind,
He knows he has the cogging to astound.
Go faster now! Your wooden gears can take it!

Old Wind Man, with your paddles whirling round!

Gary Bills

28th November

A November Memory

I remember when the days turned cold
And gentle snowflakes began to fall
I put on my scarf, gloves and boots
As the mysteries of the wood began to call

I took a walk through the woods that day
Through the snow, wrapped up all warm
Just a timid deer and a chirpy robin for company
As it was the breaking of the dawn

I stayed awhile and marvelled at the beauty
And the peace I found in the scenery that day
And whilst no one was there to see me
I ran, I laughed - I was at play

As the day got later
I decided to head home for tea
I sat by the fire, warming my hands
Then it was off to bed for me

I hoped the snow would still be there tomorrow
As I curled up in my bed
I closed my eyes, to sleep, to dream
With thoughts of my snowy day filling my head.

Claire Tupholme

29th November

Little Robin

I looked out of my window and what did I see
It had snowed all night
Everything was covered in white
I thought about my robin friend
Who used to visit me in the spring
He would sit on our hedge
And would hide under his little wing
But I had not seen him for a while and was feeling sad
Had my friend found a new home?
I hope he was safe and well, I hope he wasn't lonely
Only time would tell.

A couple of days later when the snow had melted
I looked out of my window and couldn't believe my eyes
Oh it was a wonderful surprise
On the bench stood my robin friend and he was chirping as loud as could be
I was glad he was back again and he was as happy as could be
I rushed back in to get him some crumbs
And when I went back outside there was not just one robin but four
I realised my robin now had his own family
How wonderful I cried and danced around the floor.

Oh robin, oh robin, as pretty as can be, please still come back and visit me.

Kathryn Cook

A Little Bull!

A jolly Hippopotamus
Said, 'This is very ominous,
A little Bull adorable
Has caught a cold incurable.
Bless my soul! What shall we do
If treatment's not available?'

'Fear not!' exclaimed a Nonny-Mouse,
'Take him to a coffee house,
And get some toddy hot enough
To cure his beastly tickly cough.'
'Oh, that sounds very sensible,'
Said Hippo: 'Most commendable.'

But crafty greedy Crocodile
Said, 'This is inexcusable,
I'll cure our little Bully Bull
Of ailments quite invincible.'

But thoughts of saucy Crocodile
Snapping at his valuables,
Made Bully, who's excitable
And clearly *not* expendable,
Snort - 'This is quite intolerable!'
And charged with all his might.

The moral of this story is:
Don't inflame a Bull!

Margaret Carl Hibbs

1st December

Nursery School

I don't want to go
Don't send me there please
I'm begging to stay home
I'm down on my knees

Oh come on, you'll enjoy it
You'll make lots of friends
I'm sure you'll be smiling
When every day ends

Mr Men painted
On the nursery school's door
Often sand from the sand box
Ends up on the floor

We play with the water tub
Then eat custard creams
Sometimes for games
We're split into teams

We drink orange squash
Before having a story
Some kids fall asleep
One we call Snorey

I'm four years old now
And my uniform's black
I hate infant school more
I want to go back.

Dan McPheat

2nd December

The Bumpkin

The Bumpkin is a funny thing, with purple hair and eyes of string,
That whizz and whirr and blink and stare,
It's always gone, but always there,
Around a corner peeping back, he whistles tunes between the cracks
of paving stones of green and grey,
And all the time you watch it play a mixed-up game of oddity
that then becomes reality,
The more it dances to the tune with lightning skips
and hoots and shouts,
The more I cheer and laugh and sing
The Bumpkin is a funny thing.

The Bumpkin is a funny thing, with flaying arms and clothes
that cling to each and every bony part,
Its bright red ears and yellow nose light up to show it where it goes,
Its flapping feet are never still, it hops down dale and skips up hill,
as if it always knows the drill.
Within its world it is the king,
The Bumpkin is a funny thing.

The Bumpkin is a funny thing, its teeth play notes and help it sing,
Each one a special kind of sound, you'll hear it when
it comes around,
The wild-eyed look of fearless poise, before you see it hear the noise,
A wondrous whistling, wandering wail,
It gorges pumpkin, slushes ale
And so take heed right through to spring,
The Bumpkin is a funny thing.

Shelley Fairclough

A Rational Fear Of Sharks

I'm hiding from a shark
I do hope he can't see me
I just took a photograph
Of him in a bikini

What would all the fishes say
If this print were to get out?
The hard man of the ocean
Would soon lose all his clout.

He was standing by a rock pool
Admiring his reflection
When I heard him utter to himself
'This two-piece is perfection!'

So I thought I'd take a photo
Of this maneater at ease
But now this shark is after me
'Cause I shouted out, 'Say cheese!'

So I'm hiding from a shark
This killer from the sea
And though he wears a swimsuit
He still looks fierce to me.

Jim Staton

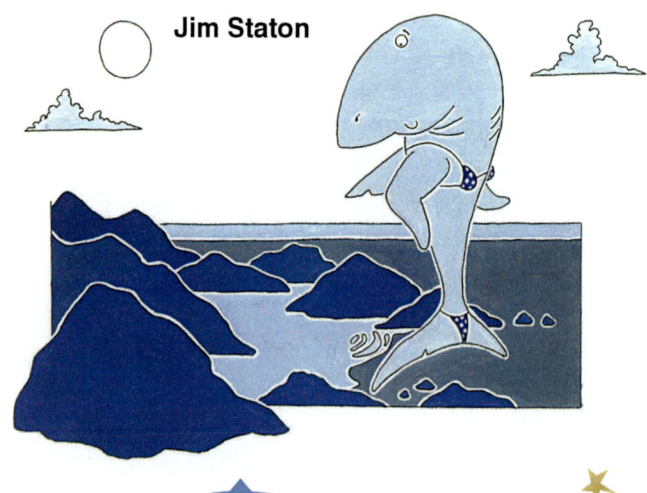

 4th December

A Child's Bedtime Prayer

Snowflakes fall against the window
Robins shelter in the shed
Please dear God let me be thankful
For my warm and cosy bed.

Thank you for a loving mother
Who cares and feeds me day by day
Teachers, friends who always help me
Directing me on the narrow way.

For these things I am so thankful
I pray for those who do not see
Fruit or bread upon the table, for them
An ever empty granary.

Keep me safe and leave me never
Some day, Lord
I hope to be
Gracious, helpful, courageous
Standing tall to honour Thee
God bless me,
   Amen.

Frances Gibson

5th December

Nagooti

Nagooti lived in the Arctic,
In the land of the ice and snow,
And the land where he lived was a crystal land
Where few men dared to go.

He didn't live in a wooden house
Or a brick one like you and me,
And he didn't know what wood was,
For he'd never seen a tree.

If his friends asked him to come for a meal,
His table manners were shocking!
He'd gulp down food, give a giant belch,
Then leave without even talking.

He loved the frozen crystal land,
And the crystal land loved him.
And they sang of their love in the midnight sun
Where the daylight never went dim.

He loved to follow the ice floes
As they made their way to the sea,
And sometimes he'd jump on a big one
And catch a ride for free.

He'd feel the wind on his whiskers,
And a smile would break on his face,
Then he'd jump just in time for safety
As the ice floe broke up without trace.

His friends were the folks of the crystal land
And he had few enemies.
He only feared the great white bear
That lived on the ice by the sea.

He'd race through the ice with the Arctic fox
But he couldn't run as fast.
His legs were too short and his feet were *huge*
So he always came in last.

 **5th December**

Sometimes he'd see a martin move,
Snow-white against white snow,
And he'd try to get a closer look,
But he always moved too slow.

He loved to watch the Arctic tern
As it dropped from the air for a fish,
And he envied the bird the easy way
Of catching the tasty dish.

But Nagooti never went hungry,
For he always fed from the sea,
And his coat was of the warmest fur,
For he was a seal, you see!

Leon Rafnson

6th December

Sleeping Child

Where stars shoot with all their might,
Where unicorns start their gentle flight,
And fishermen sing so soft and light,
I'll send my sleeping child,
Goodnight.

Jessica Shakespeare

 7th December

Blood Brothers

Amos and Andy Mosquito
Were brothers born on the same day
While Amos was born in a road ditch
Sweet Andy was born in the hay.
As time went by, old Amos, like a vampire
Sucked much blood
Poor Andy's limbs were lifeless
As on and on he trod.
Andy thought his luck had changed though
When he stumbled on a hand
Which was attached to a human body
Sprawled across the land
He gorged himself with abandon
While the man lay fast asleep
The scene was oh, so touching
It was enough to make you weep.
At this point old Amos was picking up the scent
And in next to no time
Into overdrive he went
Of course Amos and Andy Mosquito
Didn't know they were at the same sting
Until Andy coughed and spluttered
Splattering blood on Amos' wing
As recognition dawned upon them
That they were brothers true and true
They embraced each other tearfully
Their reunion overdue
But what they didn't realise
And neither of them knew
The man had infected blood
Which produced a lethal goo.
In the end both Amos and Andy
With both their distinctive charms
Sat in peace together
And died in each other's 'arms' . . .

Jim Gordon

 **8th December**

The Creepy House

The house has lain empty
For more than a year
The last occupants
Moved out in fear

The house is haunted
They all have said
By an evil spirit
Back from the dead

It climbs the stairs
In the dead of night
And creeps in your room
When you turn out the light

You know it's there
You can smell its odour
And as you breathe it in
The room feels colder

Your senses are alive
You hear every sound
Your body is frozen
You feel spellbound

It now watches you
And reads your mind
The fear you're feeling
It will need to find

You then hear it leave
As it slams shut the door
And thuds down the stairs
Then comes back for more.

Kevin McSkelly

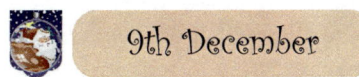 9th December

Grandpa Bert

Grandpa Bert was quite old,
and smelt slightly of mould.
He would only eat soup and drink cider.
Grandpa Bert had a box
that was covered in locks.
No one knew what was hiding inside her.

One day as he slept, we silently crept
to the box, which we took off his lap.
In our hearts we were hoping
to get the box open
before Grandpa finished his nap.

We struggled for minutes
to try and get in it
but nothing would set the lid free.
Then finally *crack* - the lid flew right back
and we all crowded forward to see.

There in the light was a startling sight,
we all stared in stunned disbelief.
For staring right back
was a small wooden rack
and on it, were Grandpa's false teeth.

When Grandpa Bert woke
he started to choke
at the sight of his full set of gnashers.
He'd been sick of the soup - that thick runny gloop -
and was longing for fried bacon rashers.

Only then did he tell
his sorrowful tale
of the day that his box lid had stuck.
He gave up the fight, but now he could bite -
he never again wants to suck.

Julie Channer

10th December

'Whatif' Land

(To Becky and Emily with love from Nanna and Irene)

What would we do if it rained lemonade
And you could eat a chocolate flower?
If it snowed vanilla ice cream
Every time we had a snow shower?
Just to think, when you got hungry
You needn't go home for a meal
You'd just bend down and pick something up
Just think how good it would feel
If you could eat orange dandelions
And pick up a leaf tasting lime
Wouldn't it be like a dream come true?
You needn't go home on time
For you'd never be hungry for dinner
And you'd never want your tea
If you wanted something to eat
You could pick it right off a tree
I suppose it would be good for some things
But if we had lemonade rain
We'd all end up rather sticky
And a bath wouldn't be the same
So I think God knows what He's doing
When He gives us fresh water to drink
And it's nice to sit round a table to eat
Egg, bacon and big sausage link
In a sandwich with plenty of sauce on
Feeling lovely and warm in your hand
Yes, I think He knows what He's doing
And I'm glad that I live in this land.

Irene Pickering

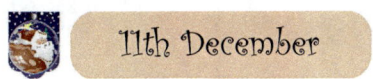
11th December

New Elf For Santa

If you wake up on Christmas Eve's night, to look to see
That you can catch Santa putting presents by the tree,
Then you'll be taken for a ride in his sleigh,
To his grotto, in a land far away.
Locked up in a stable like a prisoner you'll stay,
Until the end of the elves' Christmas holiday.
Then you will get a uniform, beard and pointed ears
And work very hard for many years.
You'll be packing presents or stacking shelves,
Alongside Santa and his many elves.
So when you go to bed on Christmas Eve's night,
Make sure from him you're out of sight.
Just stay in bed, even if you are awake
So it's only the cake you left him that he'll take.

Andy Pitcher

12th December

A Teddy Bear

I am a big fat teddy bear
I sit upon the shelf
look down on all the other toys
my owner must have wealth

My ears are getting floppy
and my knees are rather worn
my coat is getting thinner
through all the wear and tear I've borne

Although it's not surprising
as I'm over eighty years old
my foot feels as if it's got gout
and I'm sure I've caught a cold

Now Johnny's taking me off the shelf
I wonder what we will play today
will it be cowboys and Indians?
That's a game he likes to play

Sometimes we listen to music
all that pop noise hurts my head
thump, thump, thump all day long
I'm glad to go back to bed

But I like it best when he cuddles me
he's only eight years old, you know
we both asleep together a lot
off to the Land of Nod we go

We have many thrilling adventures
always together, don't you see?
I just think the world of him
and I know he will always be there for me.

Owen Robert Cullimore

13th December

Christmas At The Zoo

I was walking through the zoo one day, and quietly listening in.
The animals were shouting and making such a din.
It seemed there was a ballot, and they were trying to decide,
who was the most important, in whom they could take pride.
The wild boar was grunting loudly, and the lions roaring too,
but the elephant looked on and said, 'I'm bigger than any of you.'
The mouse said to the elephant, 'You cannot go by size,
because if you were in a boat, you know it would capsize.'
The hyenas just laughed and walked away, then the tigers
decided to have their say. 'We are fierce and make you fear
so just watch out what you say in here.'
In then joined the chimpanzee, 'Now listen all of you to me.'
Yes, every animal had their say, but they called the little donkey
silly and chased him away. And so the argument went
on, to whom does the title then belong?
A little girl came walking by, and this little donkey she did spy.
The animals were so amazed when this little girl the donkey praised.
'Little donkey you were chosen that Christmas long ago,
to carry the mother of Jesus, who had no place to go.
A silly donkey never, a humble beast that's true
Because you helped the Saviour, the title I give to you.'

Shirley Franklin

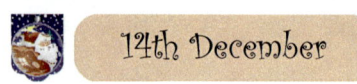 14th December

The Magic

As we climbed aboard
The wooden box
Our John, Michael, Teddy and me
That won't fly! They all shouted with glee.

But we knew the words
Full of magic you know
That would make our
Flying machine go.

We said our goodbyes
Then off we went
We circled and swooped
Oh! What an event.

They came to the windows
To wave us goodbye
Then over the playground
We went with a cry.

Then we flew through the sky
Leaving sparks as we went
And the moon as it rose
Gave us light to descend.

We chattered and laughed
As we landed at home
And told of the fun
That we'd had at Toytown.

We'd go there again
Some time when it's right
We murmured to Mum
As she tucked us up tight.

Some time! When the magic is right
Then again we can fly through the night.

Joan May Wills

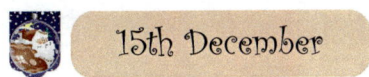 15th December

Meet The Creeps

(This poem was written for Harvey by his auntie Jackie on 30/12/05)

Mr Creep is far from sweet
He's got three legs and smelly feet.

Mrs Creep is the creepy queen
Her knees are blue and her hair is green.

Teeny Creep likes to peep
So he always wins at hide-and-seek.

The creepiest three you'll ever meet,
The creepy Creeps from Creepy Street.

Jackie Williams

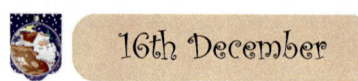 16th December

Early Learning

I went to a Christmas party, the annual family 'do',
And it wasn't the first one I'd been to, even though I am only two.
There were relatives hugging and kissing, each other and Mummy and me,
And I clung onto Mummy tightly, affixing myself to her knee.

I'd just learned the parts of the body, and we turned it into a game,
And I poked Mummy's nose and her ear and her head and called each by its right name.
Then I spotted another toddler, a cousin about age three,
And decided to get down and play with him when he toddled over to me.

I'd just learned the parts of the body, so I poked his eye and said, 'Eye.'
But he didn't seem to want to play this game, and just stood there and started to cry.
Then he lifted his arm and he thumped me, quite hard once or twice on the head,
And I changed my mind about playing with him and cried for my mummy instead.

I searched the house trying to find her; I looked into every face,
And I started to fear when she didn't appear, so I hollered and screamed down the place.
Then someone took me to Nana, and I love Nana very much too,
But this was the sort of occasion when only a mummy would do.

So Nana took me to Mummy, and I told my mummy: 'Hurt head,'
And Mummy rubbed it and kissed it, 'There, there now - all better,' she said.
And when I was feeling much better, I watched all the kids having fun,
And I slipped down off Mummy's knee to join in when I spotted a cousin aged one.

Janet Greenwood

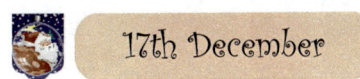 17th December

The Spot . . .

My aunt came to visit our house one day,
I'd never seen her before.
I was quite excited when the doorbell rang,
So I rushed to open the door.

'Oh, you must be Reece,' she said with a smile,
'I'm your long-lost auntie called Rose.'
And how it just missed me when she went to kiss me,
Was this enormous great spot on her nose.

I stumbled to speak when I looked at the peak,
Of the mountain that sat on her nose.
It was red round the sides and white at the top,
On a dark night it probably glows.

'Excuse me Aunt Rosie for being quite nosy,
And pardon the pun if you please.
But that thing on your face looks quite out of place,
If you bend down I'll give it a squeeze.'

'Oh, don't worry my dear,
That mound's been there for years.
It's now part of my features you see.'
'Well, until it's removed, or somehow improved,
You're certainly not kissing me . . .'

R M Hughes

18th December

Who's Santa?

Mummy, I'm confused!
Is that Santa over there?
Looking rather skinny
With funny, fluffy hair.

Wasn't he just in Asda's?
But he doesn't look the same
His skin's a different colour
Oh, his elves aren't very tame!

Surely it can't be him?
Who's making all the toys
In his factory in Lapland
For all the girls and boys?

Mummy! There's another
In that shop over there
And one on the escalator
Clutching at a teddy bear.

Santa! Can you hear me?
Oh this is far too much to bear
I'm only four (cute I know);
Should be living without a care.

Rudolph will know the answer
Being Santa's best friend and all
When I get home from shopping
I'll get Mummy to give him a call.

Mummy. Will it be OK?
I want Christmas to be just so
With lots of presents for you and Daddy
But I'll get the most you know!

Michelle Borrett

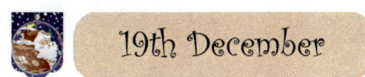 19th December

God Is Santa Claus

On the same night every year
God dresses up in red,
And converts His golden chariot
Into a reindeer-driven sled

Descending from the heavens
He fills our hearts with delight,
Bringing us His gifts of joy
He brings us love and light

Skimming across our rooftops
He glides into our dreams,
And fills our children's faces
With sun and moonlight beams

In remembrance of His Son
Who once came down to Earth,
God makes this our special day
To celebrate Jesus' birth.

Ashley O'Keefe

20th December

The Elephant's Cold

The elephant had a terrible cold,
His head was full of disease.
I asked him why some trees had collapsed,
And he cried, *'It's because I sneezed!'*

I could understand his depression,
And you'd sympathise too, I suppose,
When you learn that the hankie I gave him
Wouldn't even cover his nose!

I inquired if he had been silly,
Like playing outside in the rain
Without first putting his coat on,
Because he does that now and again.

Did he, indeed, wear his wellies,
And the scarf that I gave him last year?
But the elephant couldn't remember;
His cold made him feel very queer.

So I told him he must see our doctor
Who would prescribe a miracle cure.
Then his coughing and sneezing would vanish,
And he'd feel much better, I'm sure.

*'You must take these tablets each mealtime,
And this wonderful medicine too,'*
Said the doctor upon seeing the elephant,
'If you want to be cured of the 'flu.'

The brave elephant soon became healthy,
Having done as the doctor had told
But now it's my nose that's running,
Oh, I must have caught the elephant's cold!

Alan Hawthorn

20th December

 21st December

Topsy-Turvey Christmas

It's Christmas time again
The snow is falling down.
Its flakes are made of sugar
And are coloured chocolate-brown.
There's snowmen without hats on,
Dogs with ten-foot tails
And Santa's sleigh with bells on
Is pulled by killer whales.
Christmas trees lean sideways
And monkeys live within.
They swing from branch to branch
And they make an awful din.
Holly is not prickly,
Bells don't make a sound.
Baubles on the Christmas trees
Are triangular, not round.
There's turkeys playing football
Against the Three Wise Men.
They play with rolled-up stuffing
And the referee's a hen.
Cats sing Christmas carols,
Toys all come alive.
Action Men have dresses
While Barbie scuba-dives.
There's gravy over puddings
And peas are filled with cream.
In my topsy-turvy Christmas,
My topsy-turvy dream.

Bob Fiddaman

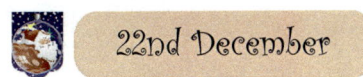 22nd December

My Invisible Aunt

My invisible aunt
Is incredibly small:
You would think when you look
That she's not there at all!

Every day when she quits
Her invisible bed,
She brushes and combs
Her invisible head.

She washes her face
With invisible soap,
And ties on her skirt
With invisible rope.

She has only invisible
Water to drink,
And she writes all her notes
In invisible ink.

She sits down for tea
On invisible chairs,
And climbs up to bed
By invisible stairs.

When she looks in the mirror
I think you'll agree
That she's wasting her time -
'Cause there's nothing to see!

Rex Andrews

23rd December

My Old Ted

My ted is old, and rather worn,
His coat is shaggy, his ear torn.
He only has one eye to see,
And doesn't have a pedigree.
I found him underneath a tree,
He was abandoned, just like me.
But he has a jolly smile,
It gives to him a certain style . . .
And I just love him, quite a lot.
Cos he's the only friend I've got.

That is not entirely true,
I have a golliwog and you.

John Owen Freeth

 24th December

Voice Market

A teacher lost her voice one day,
She had a noisy class.
So she headed to a voice market,
To find a voice to last.

The shopkeeper smiled and said, 'Hello,
Please have a little explore.
I bet you could do with a voice,
What can I do you for?'

'I need a voice to run my class
A voice that's big and strong.
Loud enough for crowds to hear
And soft to sing a song,

Sharp enough to know I'm cross
But sweet to know I'm fair,
Brave when I may feel afraid
And kind to show I care.

My class is quite a naughty lot,
I think it's fit to mention
That every time I try to teach
I strive for their attention.'

'Have you tried a megaphone?'
The market keeper said,
'Or juggling balls to teach your class,
While standing on your head?

I have just the voice for you in mind,
To help you solve your plight.
It'll cost you merely 50p,
I hope that is alright?'

And so the teacher returned to class,
With a voice sure to impress.
For when she opened up her mouth,
She had become the headmistress!

Helen Moll

25th December

'Twas The Night Before Christmas Poem

Make it snow!

'Twas the night before Christmas, when all through the house
Not a creature was stirring, not even a mouse.
The stockings were hung by the chimney with care,
In hopes that St Nicholas soon would be there.

The children were nestled all snug in their beds,
While visions of sugar-plums danced in their heads.
And Mamma in her 'kerchief, and I in my cap,
Had just settled our brains for a long winter's nap.

When out on the lawn there arose such a clatter,
I sprang from the bed to see what was the matter.
Away to the window I flew like a flash,
Tore open the shutters and threw up the sash.

The moon on the breast of the new-fallen snow
Gave the lustre of midday to objects below.
When, what to my wondering eyes should appear,
But a miniature sleigh, and eight tiny reindeer.

With a little old driver, so lively and quick,
I knew in a moment it must be St Nick.
More rapid than eagles his coursers they came,
And he whistled, and shouted, and called them by name!

'Now Dasher! now, Dancer! now, Prancer and Vixen!
On, Comet! On, Cupid! on, on Donner and Blitzen!
To the top of the porch! to the top of the wall!
Now dash away! Dash away! Dash away all!'

As dry leaves that before the wild hurricane fly,
When they meet with an obstacle, mount to the sky.
So up to the house-top the coursers they flew,
With the sleigh full of toys, and St Nicholas too.

And then, in a twinkling, I heard on the roof
The prancing and pawing of each little hoof.
As I drew in my head, and was turning around,
Down the chimney St Nicholas came with a bound.

He was dressed all in fur, from his head to his foot,
And his clothes were all tarnished with ashes and soot.
A bundle of toys he had flung on his back,
And he looked like a peddler, just opening his pack.

His eyes-how they twinkled! his dimples how merry!
His cheeks were like roses, his nose like a cherry!
His droll little mouth was drawn up like a bow,
And the beard of his chin was as white as the snow.

The stump of a pipe he held tight in his teeth,
And the smoke it encircled his head like a wreath.
He had a broad face and a little round belly,
That shook when he laughed, like a bowlful of jelly!

He was chubby and plump, a right jolly old elf,
And I laughed when I saw him, in spite of myself!
A wink of his eye and a twist of his head,
Soon gave me to know I had nothing to dread.

He spoke not a word, but went straight to his work,
And filled all the stockings, then turned with a jerk.
And laying his finger aside of his nose,
And giving a nod, up the chimney he rose!

He sprang to his sleigh, to his team gave a whistle,
And away they all flew like the down of a thistle.
But I heard him exclaim, 'ere he drove out of sight,
'Happy Christmas to all, and to all a goodnight!'

Clement Clarke Moore (1779-1863)

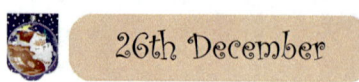

26th December

The Forgotten Present

It was early in Lapland on a frosty Christmas morn,
When the big man in red let out a long, loud yawn.
He'd safely put his reindeer each back in their cosy stall,
And was carefully pushing the sleigh against the back wall.
It was then that he noticed and let out a gasp of fright,
A present nestling in the sleigh, yet not quite out of sight.

The well-wrapped present was neither that big nor that small,
A charming precious gift, with a shape to Santa did enthral.
But how did he miss it, and to whom did it belong?
His worries continued, escalated and grew strong.
His reindeer were asleep, and his sleigh put away,
Their magic had faded with the dawning of this new day.

Over 200 million homes visited just in one night,
Children now everywhere waking with yelps of delight.
What was he to do? It had never happened before,
He'd always been so careful, so he paced around the floor.
A couple of reindeer stirred and sensed Santa's fear,
Blitzen and good old Rudolph did worryingly peer.

He calmed them back down and said all was right,
But his stomach churned constantly at the thought of his plight.
He paced once again, another half hour did pass,
'Til he finally decided to head to the workshop at last.
There was nothing more that he knew he could do,
Except get the lists of the children and go through.

A laborious task he started; a few hours did go by,
But failed to find a present-less one, though he did try.
His mind still reeling, with concern for a poor child
Who would awake this morning, all tiny, meek and mild.
The tears would roll, and the heartache begin,
They would think they deserved it for some small sin.

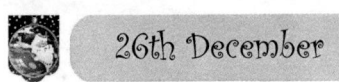 26th December

He knew he had done everything and could do no more,
When his thoughts were interrupted by a knock at the door.
It was Mrs Claus wondering why he had not come in,
For his rest, relaxation and spending time with his kin.
He apologised so sincerely, and explained all his plight,
But Mrs Claus just smiled and then laughed with delight.

'If you had read the tag,' she said, chuckling some more,
'You would have known whom the dear present was for.'
'Oh,' said the big man, who was still wearing his hat,
'I didn't think, I mean, I had never thought of that.'
So, lifting the tag, he rather carefully did read,
'To Santa, my husband, a truly wonderful man indeed!'

John Thompson

27th December

The Candy Apple Tree

In Jane's yard a candy apple tree grew,
With candy apples of red, purple and blue.
One day Jane was picking candy apples to eat,
When a candyman jumped out, landing at her feet.
He was made out of chocolate, Jane could see,
With a jiggle-jelly hat shaped like a bee.
He wore a jellybean shirt, and had bubblegum pants,
And his shirt had buttons made of maple-covered ants.

He had two candy cane eyes and a red liquorice grin,
And a candyfloss beard that hung from the tip of his chin.
'I am a candyman,' he said, 'as you can see,
And I am the protector of this candy apple tree.'
Then he flew up into the tree, quick as a cat,
And threw down a candy apple shaped like a rat.

Now every day Jane and the candyman talk about sweets,
And every day he gives her lots of candy apple treats.

Now if you should ever pick a candy apple to eat,
Prepare yourself for a candyman to land at your feet.

Rick Matiowski

 28th December

The Colour Yellow

Yellow was my colour
When I was only two,
Although my parents thought
I would look better dressed in blue.

I would grab at balloons,
Golden yellow like the sun,
I would snatch yellow balls,
Yes, snatch them and run.

The food put on my plate
Was always much too green.
Oh! How I would have liked
A dish of yellow ice cream.

I loved warm, buttered toast,
And scrambled eggs were good,
But the thing I liked the most
Was yellow custard with my pud.

Joyce Warden

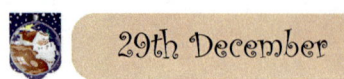
29th December

It's Snowing!

'It's snowing! It's snowing!'
    The little boy cried
Wide-eyed with excitement
    At the whiteness outside

A blanket that covers
    As far as the eye sees
So pure and new
    Even covering the trees

'Let's go for a sleigh ride!'
    He's eager and keen
Spoiling the newness
    Leaving tracks where he's been

Sliding down hills
    Making snowmen
Throwing snowballs
    At his older brother Ben

Toes tingling with cold
    He doesn't seem to care
All this fun for one small boy
    Surely, it isn't fair!

Time for bed now
    The day has been long
He'll awaken in the morning
    To find the snow has all gone

Joanne Hale

 30th December

Please

Please

Piped a small clear voice
please go over to my house
and leave a note for Santa

Please

Tell him that we've moved
there wasn't time before we left
and write in it where we've gone

Please

Can he bring the sacks
to our new home in Detroit
just in case he hasn't heard

Please

And big brother adds
say we're five hours behind now
tell him his sleigh can make it

Please

Simone Mansell Broome

 31st December

Blue Bird's Story

Blue Bird was merrily skipping home,
When she bumped into Hodgey the hedgehog,
'You look happy,' he said.
'Mouse asked me on a date to dinner,' Blue Bird said.
'Fantastic,' he said.
And off she skipped,

When she saw Olive the rabbit,
'Why, you look happy,' she said.
'Mouse asked me on a date to dinner,
And gave me a beautiful rose,' Blue Bird said.
'Fantastic,' she said.
And off she skipped.

When Frances the frog called her,
'Blue Bird, you look happy,' she said.
'Mouse asked me on a date to dinner,
Gave me a beautiful flower and then kissed me,' Blue Bird said.
'Fantastic,' she said.
And off she skipped.

When she saw Cat,
'Cat,' she called.
But Cat was not listening,
'Cat, Mouse asked me for a date to dinner,
Gave me a beautiful flower and kiss,' Blue Bird said.
'Oh nice,' said Cat.
As he licked his lips,
Smiled a satisfying smile,
And lazily walked away.
And off Blue Bird skipped,
To get ready for her dinner date.

Dawna Mechelle

Anchor Books Information

We hope you have enjoyed reading this book - and that you will continue to enjoy it in the coming years.

If you like reading and writing poetry and short stories drop us a line, or give us a call, and we'll send you a free information pack.

Alternatively, if you would like to order further copies of this book or any of our other titles, then please give us a call or log onto our website at **www.forwardpress.co.uk**
Anchor Books, Remus House, Coltsfoot Drive, Woodston,
Peterborough PE2 9JX
Tel (01733) 898102
Email anchorbooks@forwardpress.co.uk